SUCCESS WITH
ORGANIC
FRUIT

SUCCESS WITH
ORGANIC FRUIT

Yvonne Cuthbertson

GUILD OF MASTER CRAFTSMAN
PUBLICATIONS LTD

In memory of Joy Biddlecombe,
much loved and sadly missed

First published 2006 by
Guild of Master Craftsman Publications Ltd
166 High Street, Lewes, East Sussex, BN7 1XU

Text © Yvonne Cuthbertson 2006
© in the Work GMC Publications Ltd

ISBN-13 978-1-86108-483-5
ISBN-10 1-86108-483-8

British Cataloguing in Publication Data
A catalogue record of this book is available from the British Library

The right of Yvonne Cuthbertson to be identified as the author of this work
has been asserted in accordance with the Copyright Designs and Patents
Act 1988, Sections 77 and 78.

The publishers and author can accept no legal responsibility for any
consequences arising from the application of information, advice or
instructions given in this publication.

A catalogue record of this book is available from the British Library

Production Manager: Hilary MacCallum
Managing Editor: Gerrie Purcell
Editor: Alison Howard
Managing Art Editor: Gilda Pacitti
Designer: Jo Patterson
Illustrations: Penny Brown

Set in Futura

Colour origination by Altaimage
Printed and bound by Sino Publishing

FOREWORD

Oh, the joy of biting into your first strawberry of the year! My mouth waters at the thought of the sweetest dessert apples picked straight from the tree; the raspberries in summer pudding; the blackberries in blackberry and apple crumble, the ripe pears, the juicy cherries…oh, and the plums that were among the sweetest fruits I ever grew!

For most gardeners with a bit of space, growing fruiting trees, bushes and canes can become a bit of an obsession. The desire for fresh, succulent fruits picked straight from the plant, however, and the need to be pesticide-free and mindful of the environment, are frequently seen as opposing forces. How can you possibly achieve the former while maintaining the principles of the latter? I am delighted to say that you can, with the aid of this book.

Yvonne Cuthbertson has a wealth of experience growing all kinds of fruit, and here she passes on some of the secrets of her success – and all without the aid of man-made chemicals. If you pick up any old volume on fruit growing, you will see that masses of advice is given over to the plethora of pests and diseases that are likely to infect and infest your crops. Pests and diseases are attracted to fruit, perhaps more than any other garden plant group, so if you do not want to take the easy way out by blasting the bugs with something noxious, it is important to know how to grow your fruit to its optimum in terms of health. The healthier the plant, the better it is able to resist being infected. In this book Yvonne takes you through the ideal fruit-growing processes, from variety, choice and good husbandry, through to how to harvest when the crops are at their best. I have never seen organic advice on fruit-growing, such as Yvonne offers here, in such a modern, concise and easy-to-follow style. For this reason alone, the book will take a prominent place on my shelf.

GRAHAM CLARKE MIHort, FLS
Consultant contributor to *Organic Life* magazine

Contents

LEFT **Almond tree in bloom at Tantur Ecumenical Institute, Jerusalem**

ABOVE **A formal fruit garden with trees in rows**

Introduction

Organic gardening means working with nature for the benefit of man, plant and environment. It means encouraging wildlife into your garden, growing plants that attract, and companion planting. It means good husbandry, meeting your plants' needs, and looking after your soil. Most importantly, it means that your family can enjoy safe, natural, chemical-free food. Commercial fruit growers grow fruit not for flavour but for its appearance, high yields and ability to weather transportation. What could be more satisfying than growing your own fruit in a way that protects it naturally from pests and diseases?

Fruit growing has never been so easy, reliable and rewarding, so now is the time to try. There is an amazing variety to choose from, and you will be able to enjoy fruit that is far superior in flavour and quality. The sense of achievement will be rivalled only by the enjoyment of tasting your own sweet, succulent home-grown fruit. If you do not have room for a separate fruit area, do not worry. The secret is to make the most of the space available and the entire growing season. Combine fruits that let you pack more into a small space. Many new varieties are bred for their space-saving qualities, and new techniques allow them to be grown closer together so substantial yields can be produced in small areas. Mouthwatering soft fruits, perhaps just a few raspberry canes, blueberries or gooseberry bushes, can be worked into a border for an effect that is as flavoursome as it is ornamental. Fruit trees make good ornamental features, with lovely spring blossom and beautiful autumn leaves. Apple or pear trees may be too large for a small garden, but you could plant a specimen tree in the lawn or buy fruit varieties on dwarfing rootstocks and squeeze them in as cordons or espaliers. Grow vines on trellises and pergolas. Most fruit can be grown in containers, offering an enormous amount of pleasure for remarkably little effort. Try Minarette or Ballerina fruit trees, or column-shaped apples like 'Maypole'. Strawberries thrive in tubs or window boxes, lemons and oranges in pots in a conservatory or on a sunny patio, melons and apricots in the greenhouse.

Growing fruit is far less demanding than growing vegetables. Most vegetables are temporary residents, whereas fruit will be around for many years. You will need to prepare the soil carefully by digging it in winter to expose pests to the birds, incorporating well-rotted manure or compost and applying organic fertilizer, but once established, fruit trees need almost no regular care. They can be mulched to save on watering and weeding, unlike vegetable beds which must be weeded and watered constantly. Soft fruits do need to be fed, sprayed and pruned. You will need to be vigilant over pests and diseases and take remedial action. It is also wise to protect fruit from birds using netting or fruit cages.

As well as the pleasure gained from growing your own organic fruit, the methods of storing it are deliciously satisfying. Think of bottled fruits, chutneys, jellies, jams and pies lining the larder shelves, or a freezer filled with containers of luscious, ripe raspberries, blackcurrants and cherries – a selection of treats to look forward to during the long, dark days of winter.

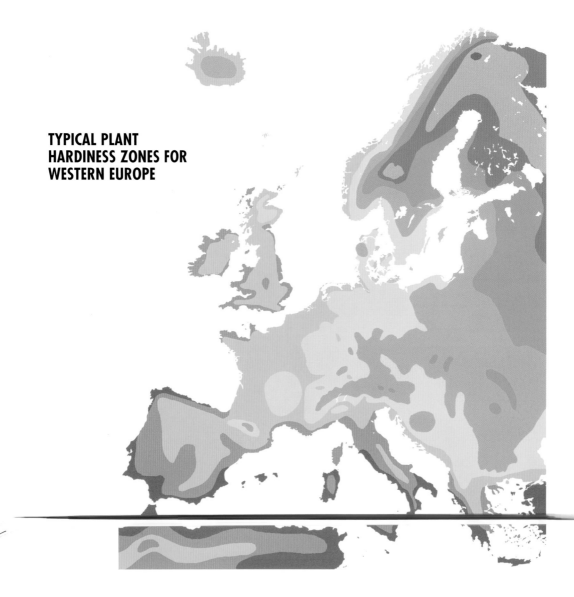

**TYPICAL PLANT
HARDINESS ZONES FOR
WESTERN EUROPE**

GROWING FRUIT ACROSS THE WORLD

Fruit can be grown in many parts of the world. Conditions in Britain are similar to those found in some parts of Europe, so the same kinds of fruit should grow there quite happily. In other areas, such as the Mediterranean, adjustments may be needed, including extra watering or planting in shade. Factors including extremes of cold and hours of sunlight must also be taken into account. Across North America, there are more extreme variations of temperature than those found across Britain and Northern Europe. To grow fruit successfully the factors that will need to be taken into consideration include the hours of cold weather in winter, how hot the summers are, and whether the climate is damp or dry. The charts on these pages should help you to determine your chances of success.

**TYPICAL PLANT
HARDINESS ZONES
FOR NORTH AMERICA**

Keys to colours (both maps)

Zone 1:   below –50°F (–46°C)

Zone 2:   –50 to –40°F (–46 to –40°C)

Zone 3:   –40 to –30°F (–40 to –34.5°C)

Zone 4   –30 to –20°F (–34.5 to –29°C)

Zone 5   –20 to –10°F (–29 to –23°C)

Zone 6   –10 to 0°F (–23 to –18°C)

Zone 7   0 to 10°F (–18 to –12°C)

Zone 8   10 to 20°F (–12 to –7°C)

Zone 9   20 to 30°F (–7 to –1°C)

Zone 10   30 to 40°F (–1 to 4°C)

Zone 11   above 40°F (above 4°C)

HOW TO USE THESE MAPS

Each entry in the plant directory lists the relevant zones where it
should be possible to grow the plant successfully, based on these
heat-zone maps. Find your location on the map, and you can then
identify the zone that your area belongs to. Do not forget to take
into account that cities are warmer than rural locations. Planting
shelter belts of trees, or planting against a sunny, south-facing wall
and/or in raised, well-drained beds, can help to give plants better
conditions in which to thrive.

11

LEFT A section of a mixed fruit
and vegetable garden

CHAPTER 1

Where to grow fruit outdoors

Most fruit is easy to grow and has played an important part in the garden through the centuries. If you have the space a separate fruit garden is ideal, but if you do not, fruit can be grown imaginatively in many different places. Most fruit trees and bushes provide colour either when in flower or bearing fruit and make an extremely ornamental and decorative addition to your garden. When planning your fruit area, take into account the minimum number of trees that will be required for pollination to occur. Position compatible cultivars near to each other to ensure the production of satisfactory crops. Remember that some fruits are self-fertile and do not need a partner.

ABOVE **Fruit ripening on a large apple tree**

LOCATION

In a large garden, there may be room to devote an area exclusively to fruit, planting rows of trees, bushes and canes, bordered by restricted fruit forms, in a formal setting. You might consider planting an informal orchard. Where space is limited and you plan to grow only a small variety of fruit, bush fruit, such as blackcurrant and strawberries, can be incorporated in the ornamental border; plum, pear and apple trees can be grown as lawn specimens, and gooseberries as a decorative double or triple cordon against a wall or fence. Fruit trees can be cultivated as espaliers, fans or cordons around the borders of the garden. Trained fruit trees can be used to decorate arches and pergolas. If many varieties are to be grown, it is a good idea to have a separate fruit area within the main garden. Here, fruits with the same requirements can be grown together. Even a small garden will support a separate fruit area, if suitable rootstocks are chosen.

ABOVE **Banana plant in container**

CHOOSING A SITE

The site you choose should be sunny and sheltered if the plants are to yield good quality, flavoursome fruit. Choose one in full sun if possible, as the fruit will always taste sweeter. Dessert fruits require more light than culinary fruits, because colour and flavour is important. Light and warmth are essential to ripen both the fruits and the wood, and to promote the development of fruit buds for next year's crop. Areas with some light shade are tolerated by early-ripening pears, apples and plums, or by bush and cane fruits including blackberries.

Plants should not be exposed to rain dripping from overhanging tree branches, and the soil should not be dry. Avoid frost-prone sites, because fruit flowers, the unopened buds and fruitlets are highly prone to frost damage. Plant fruits that need more nitrogen, such as plums, pears, blackcurrants and cooking apples, in a separate section within the fruit area. Fruit that depends more heavily on potash, including gooseberries, red and white currants and eating apples, should also be allotted their own area.

ABOVE **Fruiting blackberry canes**

16

WINDBREAKS

Fruit will grow better if it is protected from wind, which has a drying and buffeting effect. Yields can decrease by 15 per cent in gardens that are only slightly exposed to wind, and in very exposed gardens yields can be reduced by 50 per cent. Wind exposure also discourages pollinating insects, damages growth, makes fruits fall prematurely and causes irregular cropping. As altitude increases, winds become stronger and the growing season shorter.

The type of windbreak used will depend on the degree of planting. Avoid evergreen hedges and solid fences, which can block the wind and cause turbulence. Many hedge plants, for example hornbeam, can be used as screens. One disadvantage of living windbreaks is that they compete with the fruit trees for water, light and nutrients and can be host to a variety of diseases and pests. Situated in a different part of the garden, however, hedges will provide food, nesting places, and shelter for birds, and sheltered corridors for wild creatures going from garden to garden and to wild areas beyond. A mixed hedge will help to encourage wildlife into your garden. Try hawthorn mixed with a small percentage of other varieties including evergreens to provide winter cover. Fences provide cheap, instant windbreaks, but should have gaps between the slats to filter the wind. Windbreaks made from plastic netting or coir and erected on poles and wires are ideal for the smaller garden. They filter rather than block the air and can be placed where they are most needed. For the best effect they should be 3ft (90cm) high and 19ft 6in (6m) apart.

ABOVE **Screen netting can make a good temporary windbreak**

MICROCLIMATE

Conditions can vary considerably from one part of your garden to another. Altitude, latitude and the degree of exposure in different areas of your plot will all play a part in determining what types of fruit can be grown there successfully.

Before you decide what kind of fruit to plant and where to plant it, it is important to take these into consideration. The chart below covers some of the most important questions you should ask yourself before choosing:

1 What is the position of my garden in relation to the sun?

2 How much sun does each area of my garden receive at various times of the day?

3 Which areas are in sun and shade at various times of the year?

4 Is there a prevailing wind, and if so, from which direction does it come?

5 Is any part of the garden particularly windy compared to other areas?

6 Are any areas particularly exposed – for example north-facing slopes?

7 Are some parts of the garden more sheltered than others?

8 Does the drainage vary, and do any areas dry out completely in summer?

ABOVE **Using hedges as windbreaks**

WALLS AND FENCES

Solid fences, garage, outbuilding and boundary walls, trellises and pergolas, particularly those in full sun, all provide shelter from the wind and are ideal for cultivating trained fruit. A sunny, south facing wall, for instance, is an ideal spot for a fan-trained fig, cherry, apricot or gage tree. Growing fruit in this way makes good use of space and allows fruits to develop and ripen well. They are also easier to protect from frost and bird damage. Solid fences and walls give shelter and, if in a sunny position, the extra warmth reflected from them improves the quality of the fruits, aids bud development and allows you to grow more exotic fruits such as peaches and nectarines. Space against walls and fences is often limited, so choose restricted fruit forms and keep them in shape with summer pruning. Make sure that any structure you build is high enough to accommodate the variety of fruit chosen. A grape vine can be grown over a pergola or an arch, but make sure that such structures are strong enough to support heavy crops, particularly in strong winds, and that there is enough space for the plants to spread out as they grow.

ABOVE **Loganberries espaliered on a sunny wall**

ASPECT

Most fruits will thrive in a south-facing position, but the southern, south-eastern and south-western aspects are best used to grow sun-loving fruits such as grapes, gages, peaches, nectarines, cherries, plums, apples, figs, pears and apples. The soil at the base of a south-facing wall can become very dry and will need watering and mulching during the growing season.

Westerly aspects receive the afternoon sun but also the most rain. They are also exposed to south-westerly winds. Fruits including apricots, gooseberries, cherries, blackberries, nectarines, peaches, grapes, cherries, gages, raspberries, apples, and red and white currants should all succeed here.

The east receives the morning sun but it is a dry place in the garden because it is shaded in the afternoon and open to the cold easterly wind. Suitable fruits for growing in this aspect include blackberries, raspberries, cherries, apples, gooseberries, currants, plums and early pears.

Only fruits that can grow and ripen in cold situations should be grown in the north part of the garden. Cordon currants and gooseberries and blackberries, early culinary apples and fan-trained damsons are examples, though they will ripen later than those grown in the other aspects.

ABOVE **Olive trees growing in a sunny position**

PREPARATION AND PLANNING

As for any other area of your garden, you will need to draw up a plan. The keys to success are advance planning and preparation. The better your plans and site preparation, the better the results. The layout of your garden will be determined by its size, shape and nature, and, most importantly, what you want to grow. In a large garden, an area can be designated purely for fruit cultivation. If space is limited, fruit can be incorporated into the garden as a whole. Semi-dwarfing and dwarfing rootstocks can be grown in a tiny area, and a wide range of fruit can be grown provided the right rootstock and method of training is chosen for each.

What you choose will also be influenced by your budget and the climate where you live. Check whether your choice has any special needs, and take into account its preferred growing conditions and recommended planting distances. Remember that fruit trees are a permanent feature: plan the position of trees such as pears, sweet cherries and apples, carefully, planting a self sterile cultivar near a cultivar which it will cross-pollinate. It is a good idea to plan for a succession of fruits, using a wide choice of different cultivars.

ABOVE **Kumquats can be grown outdoors in warm countries or in pots under glass**

PLANNING THE FRUIT AREA

Consult catalogues and your family to decide what to grow. If your garden is small, decide where you will grow your chosen fruit and what forms it will take, including restricted fruit forms.

1 Work out the eventual size of the mature fruit plants you have chosen and how much space you will need to grow them.

2 Draw your plan to scale on graph paper, marking in features such as the greenhouse, compost heap, cold frame and walk-in polytunnels. Mark in trees, walls, hedges and bonfire or incinerator site.

3 Divide your design into sections, bearing in mind the growing requirements of each cultivar.

4 Indicate rows or blocks of fruit plants, allowing for spacing between them. Avoid overplanting – one apple, plum, or cherry tree will be enough for a family.

5 On level ground, run rows north to south to ensure the plants get the maximum amount of sunlight. If you intend to plant on a slope, let the rows follow the contours of the hill.

6 Mark in the paths. Consider how you are going to supply water.

FRUIT GARDEN DESIGNS

The fruit garden you are planning must be practical, and it will certainly be useful, but that does not mean that it cannot be beautiful. The suggestions on these pages show two very different kinds of fruit garden, but I hope they will inspire you to plan one that fits your exact needs and requirements. The regular lines of a more formal fruit garden should appeal to anyone with a sense of order.

In the design below, rows of bushes and canes are spaced regularly across the plot. A line of autumn-fruiting raspberries can look effective when they are grown as an ornamental divider. The garden has been framed on three sides using fruit trees trained in fans, espaliers and cordons. A low step-over forms the fourth border and ensures that the fruit area is a real feature of the whole garden.

A FORMAL FRUIT GARDEN LAYOUT

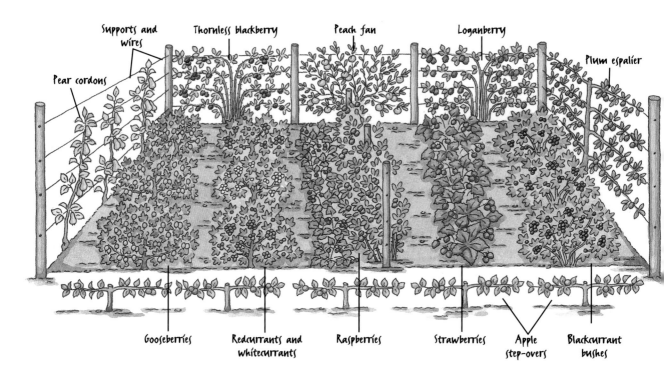

ABOVE **A formal fruit garden layout with fruit growing in rows and trained into precise shapes**

AN INFORMAL LAYOUT

A well-planned fruit garden can be just as tempting a place to linger as any other area of the garden. A pergola with a grape vine growing over it looks attractive, and you might also want to place some seating below the shady vine, so that after all your hard work you can sit back and admire – quite literally – the fruits of your labours. An informal layout might include a wall with a loganberry espaliered against it, gooseberry bushes, apple cordons, plum fans, raspberry canes and currant bushes. Pot-grown citrus fruits look attractive, and a large potted kumquat is an effective focal point. Incorporate companion plants like nasturtiums, marigold, petunias and garlic, and edge with strawberries or alpine strawberries.

AN INFORMAL FRUIT GARDEN LAYOUT

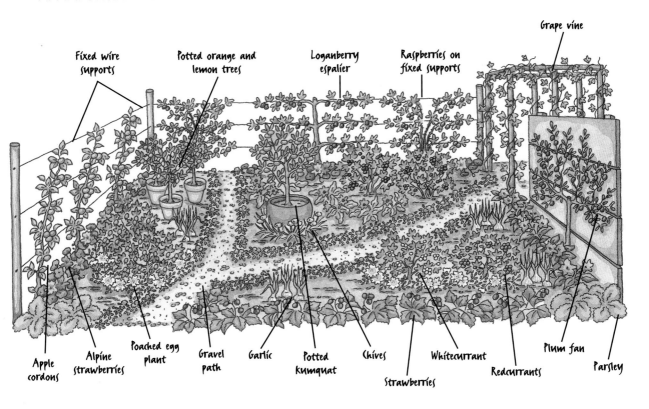

Fixed wire supports • Potted orange and lemon trees • Loganberry espalier • Raspberries on fixed supports • Grape vine

Apple cordons • Alpine strawberries • Poached egg plant • Gravel path • Garlic • Potted kumquat • Chives • Strawberries • Whitecurrant • Redcurrants • Plum fan • Parsley

ABOVE **An informal fruit garden layout with a profusion of fruit and flowers in a colourful array**

POTAGERS

Potager is the French word for kitchen garden, and is essentially an ornamental vegetable garden in which herbs and fruit are also grown. Crops are chosen for their aesthetic appeal as well as their flavour, and a potager can be a glorious riot of colourful plants and foliage.

The layout of a potager is similar to that of a parterre, with formal beds and geometric patterns. Traditionally, the shape is rectangular. The geometric design depends largely on colourful planting for visual appeal, but height can add extra interest. A potager usually has a focal point, such as a large feature plant grown in a container, where the paths meet in the centre. A citrus tree in a terracotta pot is a good choice: try the lemon-mandarin hybrid *Citrus x meyeri*, commonly known as Meyer's lemon, which is slow-growing. Cane wigwams of vegetables, herbs or fruit are also effective.

The beds of a potager can be raised or at ground level, though the former allows for ease of cultivation and access. Arches covered with climbing vines can also be used. Diagonal planting will add to the aesthetic value, and a companion-planted flower border of marigolds and nasturtiums will deter pests. Site your potager so that it backs on to a sunny wall against which you can grow espaliered fruit trees such as loganberries. The whole potager can be surrounded by a step-over apple hedge.

AN ORNAMENTAL POTAGER

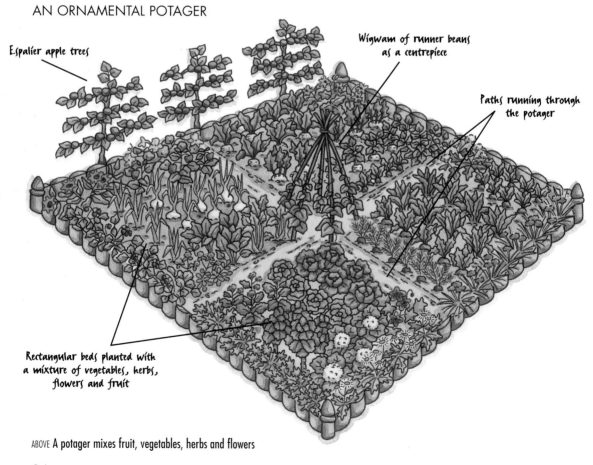

Espalier apple trees

Wigwam of runner beans as a centrepiece

Paths running through the potager

Rectangular beds planted with a mixture of vegetables, herbs, flowers and fruit

ABOVE **A potager mixes fruit, vegetables, herbs and flowers**

PROTECTING YOUR CROPS

Soft fruits can suffer from bird damage, so if you have space, build a fruit cage. There are several easily-assembled kit varieties available, in almost any size that might be required. These comprise a light, tubular, aluminium frame with a door, over which lightweight, plastic netting is fitted. You can also make your own frame from timber. Make sure the head height is no lower than 6ft (2m) to allow you to walk inside. Low fruit cages about 12in (30cm) high can be useful for protecting strawberry plants.

Strawberries and other crops can be planted through slits in black polythene, which protects them from pests such as slugs. They should also crop earlier. Use polythene sheeting and slit holes at the normal planting distances. Plant as shown in the diagram below.

Netting is also useful. Make sure that the mesh size will keep out small birds, but will not trap their legs – between half an inch (12mm) and ¾in (18mm) across is ideal.

ABOVE **A whitecurrant protected with netting**

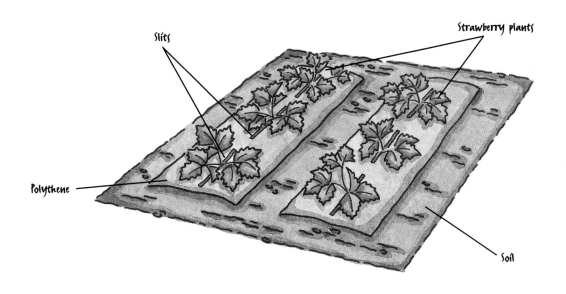

ABOVE **Fruit can be grown through slits in polythene**

FRUIT IN CONTAINERS

The popularity of growing fruit in containers has grown in recent years. If you do not have enough space to grow all the fruit you require, many fruits will succeed in containers, as long as they are watered and fed regularly to maximise yields. This idea has grown in popularity in recent years. Apart from the fact that they look ornamental and attractive, there can be positive benefits to growing produce in containers. Crops can be moved round easily to catch the sun or to protect them from the cold. There will also be fewer soil pests to contend with, and it will be easy to adjust the compost and drainage to suit the various plants.

You will need to pay special attention to planting, watering, feeding and potting on, particularly if you intend to grow fruit trees. Containers are also particularly useful for plants that would not survive in the ground. For example, lime-hating cultivars can be container cultivated if your soil is chalky. But remember to water these with rain water as tap water can often be as limy as the soil.

There is a huge range of containers to choose from, but for the best results, choose your container bearing in mind the needs of the plant you are intending to grow. A large container at least 15in (37.5cm) deep will accommodate cherry, plum, pear and apple trees, all of which need a free root run. But, choose your varieties carefully. If it is your intention to grow a single apple tree, for instance, you will need to buy a dwarf rootstock such as M27 or M9 which has three or four compatible varieties grafted on to it, negating the need for further fruit trees for pollination. Avoid shallow containers as the roots will not have enough depth, which will result in either the compost drying out very quickly, or becoming waterlogged. All fruits will crop well in good quality multipurpose compost, but this can prove expensive in large quantities. It is cheaper to buy growing bags and tip out the contents, or to add up to half the volume of garden topsoil to the compost. For the organic gardener, home-made compost from the compost heap is both ideal and cost free.

ABOVE **Maypoled orange in container**

CHOOSING POTS AND TUBS

Your choice of pots will probably be influenced by your budget. Plastic pots are inexpensive, lightweight, easy to store and clean, and they will not crack when the nights become frosty. Their water content can be judged just by lifting them. Remember to make drainage holes before adding the plants. Mock-terracotta pots that are made from polypropylene give an authentic appearance of terracotta and provide insulation for the compost.

Clay and terracotta pots are more expensive than plastic, and heavier to move around. They also dry out faster, so they will need to be watered more frequently. A good water-conserving solution is to line them with polythene before planting. Soak new terracotta pots in water for 24 hours before using.

Glazed earthenware pots are made in a huge range of colours and design, and the glazing helps to prevent water loss. Not all glazed pots have drainage holes, so check carefully before buying.

Concrete pots are available in a variety of designs and mouldings. They are stable and frost-resistant, but they can be heavy to move around. They may look rather stark at first, but will look more attractive as they 'weather', though this can take a long time.

Reconstituted stone pots are made from ground-up, moulded stone. They also take a while to weather and are very heavy to move around, but are both frost-resistant and stable.

Wooden half barrels make stunning containers for mixed displays, and they are stable and frost-resistant. They can be bought as replicas, although some replicas have plywood bases and inferior metal bands, making their lifespan a short one. They may also fall apart if they are allowed to dry out, and you will probably need to drill drainage holes in them before planting.

Fibreglass containers are expensive, but modern and stylish with a high gloss finish. They come in a variety of colours, but can crack or shatter if knocked. They are more stable than plastic pots, frost-resistant, and are relatively easy to move around.

ABOVE **Mock-terracotta strawberry pot**

POTS AND TUBS

When planting pots and tubs, use a mixture of two-thirds multipurpose compost and a third of grit. Ensure good drainage by placing a deep layer of hardcore, which also adds weight and stability, at the bottom. Place large pieces over the drainage holes, then a layer of smaller pieces on top to a depth of at least 1in (2.5cm). Layer peat, peat substitute or pulverized bark over the hardcore to stop the compost washing away. Place a layer of compost about 3in (7.5cm) deep over the peat or bark. Containers can be lined with plastic sheeting to conserve water, or cut the bottom off a plastic bottle, upturn it and sink it into the compost to allow water to penetrate the plant roots.

Informal planting is better than a regimented look. Set tubs or troughs in their final positions before filling and planting, then walk around the container and view it from all angles. Fill the container to within 1in (2.5cm) of the top and dig planting holes using a trowel. After planting, water well to help to settle the compost, using a fine rose, and water the foliage to remove any soil particles. Water in the shade as sun on the wet leaves may damage them.

MAINTENANCE

Check and water your containers even after rain, because the 'umbrella' of leaves prevents the rain from reaching the compost, which can result in the plants beginning to wilt quite quickly. Never allow your pots and tubs to dry out or to become waterlogged, and always keep a full can of water to hand so that the water you use is at the same temperature as the atmosphere. Apply an organic liquid feed once a fortnight during summer.

WINDOW BOXES

Window boxes are available in various materials, including terracotta, plastic and wood, which can be painted or stained to complement the style of your house. Check that the fixing used for your window box is strong and secure enough to take its weight when full.

UNUSUAL CONTAINERS

Recycled household objects can make effective and free containers. Try using an old galvanised bucket, or perhaps an old pair of boots to make a real talking point.

LEFT **A pair of old boots makes an unusual and attractive container**

HANGING BASKETS

Hanging baskets are the perfect way to add height to any planting scheme and provide immediate impact. There are plastic-coated wire baskets, plastic ones, or even clay pots held in rope nets. A round-bottomed wire basket is a popular choice. It can be lined with a variety of materials, from traditional moss to pre-formed wood fibre liners. Wool 'moss' liner is an ideal substitute for natural moss, is suitable for any shaped basket, and has excellent water retaining properties. Try planting strawberries with parsley, which looks attractive and is an ideal companion plant.

Plant parsley in a hanging basket

Add some strawberry plants

Fill the liner with compost

Plant the top of the basket

The finished companion-planted basket

CONTAINER PLANTING

For successful cultivation, always choose fruits with a proven record for container growing. Figs like their roots restricted, so they are ideal; try planting 'Brown Turkey'. Strawberries are an all-time favourite. Growing them in a container such as a strawberry barrel with side planting holes keeps them free from slug damage and they will not need mulching like crops grown in the ground. 'Evita' has good mildew resistance and flavour and crops in early to mid-season. Try planting strawberries and parsley together in a hanging basket. See the table below for a few of the many fruits that grow well in containers.

ABOVE **An olive tree can be grown in a container.**

SUITABLE CONTAINER FRUITS

Blackcurrants 'Baldwin' (a compact variety)

Cherry 'Stella'

Calamondin orange (also available in variegated form)

Dessert apples 'Discovery' with 'Sunset'

Gooseberry 'Leveller' or 'May Duke'

Mandarin orange

Grape vines (grow in large tubs)

Lemon 'Meyer'

Olive 'Arbequina'

Pomegranate 'Nana'

Peach 'Terrace Amber'

THE ORNAMENTAL BORDER

If you have no space for a separate fruit garden, a wide range of fruits can be grown in the ornamental border. Alpine strawberries look delightful in borders or as an edging. They are easy to raise from seed, and if they are sown under glass from mid-winter to early spring, the plants should be large enough to plant out by early summer, and will produce berries from mid-summer to late autumn in the first year. Try 'Golden Alexandria', which has attractive, golden foliage early in the year and sweet fruit.

Gooseberries, redcurrants and blackcurrants are all excellent choices for the ornamental border, and are widely available from nurseries.

ABOVE **Blackcurrants can be grown in the ornamental border**

ABOVE **A wide range of container grown fruit at the nursery**

CHAPTER 2

Cultivating fruit under cover

The productivity of the fruit area can be increased dramatically in cooler climates if crops are grown in a protected environment. In cooler climates, growing seasons are shorter, and the shorter the growing season the more effective cover is likely to be. If you grow crops under cover, air and soil temperatures are higher than outside and the crops are sheltered from the wind, all of which prolongs the growing season. The quality and yield of many plants is also improved by higher temperatures and shelter. Remember that any plants grown under cover must be gradually hardened off before being exposed to outside conditions or they may suffer a setback.

ABOVE **A small greenhouse in a corner of the garden**

GREENHOUSES

One of the chief benefits of a greenhouse is the extra warmth and shelter it will offer your plants. Cultivating fruit in a greenhouse will not only extend its growing season, but also ensure its survival, which may not be assured if it is grown outside. When protected from frost, winds, rain and pests such as birds, fruit thrives and ripens easily, and out-of-season cultivars flourish. Most tree and soft fruits may be grown under glass and nectarines and peaches can be trained as fans. Vines benefit from the shelter, though it is best to plant the rootstock outside and train it into the greenhouse through an opening in the side.

Greenhouses are an asset to any garden, large or small, and come in a huge variety of shapes and sizes. The protection offered will give you the flexibility to grow and harvest a larger variety of fruits. You will need to install a support system for climbing plants. This can be done by stretching wires up to the ridge of the greenhouse, then tying canes to the wire behind each plant.

It is best to pot or plant hardy fruits that will be grown in the greenhouse in autumn, then keep them cool. Fruit trees need plenty of fresh air, so leave the ventilators – and on warm days the door – open, unless frost or high winds are forecast. In early winter, bring in any potted fruit plants from the previous season and mulch trees in the greenhouse borders with well-rotted manure or compost. Turn the heat on after a few weeks and adjust it or turn it off as necessary, making sure there is always some ventilation. As the weather becomes hotter, spray and damp down the floors and staging daily and check regularly for any build-up of pests. When the flowers of the fruits begin to open, spray and damp down on sunny days. Continue when the fruit has formed, making sure the plants never lack water. When the fruits begin to ripen stop spraying, but after picking start again and continue until autumn. When all the fruit has been harvested, place potted trees outside. Repot them in autumn every year.

ABOVE **Greenhouse roof vents are essential for ventilation**

CHOOSING A GREENHOUSE

Even a small greenhouse will make a difference to the number of plants you can grow, and the initial cost will be recovered many times over. Buy the largest you can afford and for which you have the space. Aluminium is cheaper and virtually maintenance free; it is also easy to construct. Wood costs more but looks natural and retains more heat. Wooden greenhouses, however, are high on maintenance. The most usual design is free-standing with glass sides and a pitched roof. It can be sited anywhere and is inexpensive and practical. A lean-to greenhouse is another good option as a wall forms half of the structure and helps to reduce the cost of heating. Plants such as apricots, peaches and nectarines can be trained in fans, and fruit protected from frost ripens easily. Glass is traditional, but alternative glazing materials including rigid plastics are lighter than glass and better heat insulators.

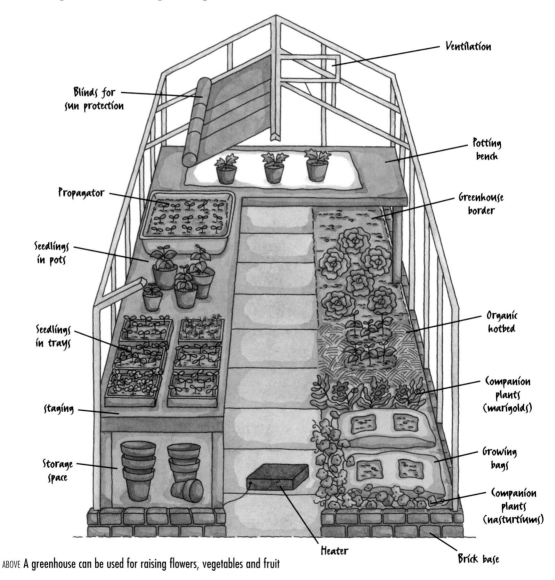

Ventilation

Blinds for sun protection

Potting bench

Propagator

Greenhouse border

Seedlings in pots

Organic hotbed

Seedlings in trays

Companion plants (marigolds)

Staging

Storage space

Growing bags

Companion plants (nasturtiums)

Heater

Brick base

ABOVE **A greenhouse can be used for raising flowers, vegetables and fruit**

HEATING

The degree to which you heat your greenhouse will depend largely on what fruit crops you want to grow. If you want to overwinter tender plants, heating will be essential. You will need a power source such as electricity, which is both reliable and clean. You might choose a thermostatically controlled heater that will switch on and off automatically. Make sure that this is installed by a qualified electrician.

Gas heaters are another option for heating greenhouses. They can also be controlled by a thermostat, but they are more expensive to run. Paraffin heaters are ideal for keeping out frost, but they are not efficient enough to use all the time. Both gas and paraffin heaters give off water vapour, which can cause condensation. Whatever method you choose, sheets of bubble polythene attached to the glazing can complement your heating system as they will help to prevent heat loss.

Choose your crops carefully according to how much you want to heat your greenhouse. The fruit you grow may have to fit in with the needs of any other produce you grow. Fruits that are suitable for growing in an unheated greenhouse include figs, grapes, peaches and early strawberries. The many fruits that can be grown in a heated greenhouse include lemons, passion fruit and kumquats.

GREENHOUSE TEMPERATURES

Cold greenhouse:
Minimum temperature a few degrees warmer than the temperature outside

Cool greenhouse:
Minimum temperature 40–45°F (5–7°C)

Warm greenhouse:
Minimum temperature 55°F (13°C)

SITING YOUR GREENHOUSE

Choose an open, sunny position for your greenhouse as warmth and maximum light are very important. The site should be open, but make sure there is some shelter from prevailing winds, such as a fence, hedge or wall, as it will will help to break their force. Do not site your greenhouse too near trees, or they will cast shade over your crops and affect growth rates and yields. In addition, falling leaves will reduce light, and they may also exude gums that will make your glazing dirty and may prove difficult to remove.

Try to make the most of the sun by ensuring that the roof ridge of your greenhouse runs from east to west, with the longest side to the south. If you choose the lean-to type of greenhouse, try to site it facing as near towards south as possible where it will receive maximum light. The wall against which it is placed will store warmth during the day and release it at night.

SOIL WARMING BENCHES

A soil warming bench is a useful greenhouse extra. Heat at the roots is more important for newly-rooted plants than warm air around the tops. Make sure that you use a weather-proof socket, which should be professionally installed. Check the type and quantity of cable you will need with an electrician.

USING THE BENCH

Keep the sand moist at all times to prevent the cable from overheating, and to ensure that the heat is transferred to the compost in the pots and trays rather than being retained in the sand.

METHOD

1 Build a wooden frame to the size required, using 1 x 6in (2.5cm x 15cm) timber, treated with a plant-friendly preservative. Drill a hole for the cable or thermostat.

2 Cover a level bench with thick polythene and add a layer of capillary matting. Place the wooden frame on top and fill it with a 1in (2.5cm) layer of moist sand.

3 Coil the cable along the length of the bench, to ensure that all areas receive some heat. There should be a space of 3–4in (7.5–10cm) between each cable to prevent overheating. When the cable is in place, cover with a further 2–3in (5–7.5cm) of soft, well-moistened sand.

A SOIL-WARMING BENCH

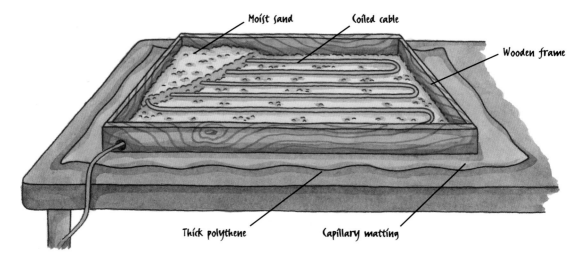

Moist sand

Coiled cable

Wooden frame

Thick polythene

Capillary matting

GREENHOUSE PROPAGATORS

Greenhouse propagators are enclosed cases, usually made from plastic, with a built-in heating element. They help to reduce costs by restricting the area to which heat is applied. Once they are set up, running costs are low. A propagator can make a great difference when you are starting off fruit seed such as melon, because faster germination is achieved. It is a vital piece of equipment if you plan to sow tender crops, such as tropical fruits, early in the season.

Keep your propagator moisture-free and wipe off any condensation that forms on the lid overnight. If left, these droplets can wet the seedlings and cause them to damp off.

ABOVE **A heated propagator for the greenhouse**

ABOVE **A commercially-produced rain barrel**

WATER

Moisture is important for greenhouse crops, but if you water your crops too much it will encourage botrytis and moulds, and too little water will encourage spider mite and mildew. Err on the side of caution during the growing season, and spray the plants, floor and glass sides of your greenhouse with a fine jet of water. Do this in the morning, which will allow it to dry before evening. It is a good idea to keep a tank of water under the staging, so that it is always at the same temperature as the greenhouse. Collect rainwater in a barrel to use on your crops. It is naturally low in salt and chlorine so it is better for them than water from the mains. Almost any large container can be used to collect water, but commercially-designed ones are usually the most convenient. They are available in various sizes, with accessories including lids to keep out insects and make them safer for children and animals.

STAGING, SHELVING AND BENCHING

Shelving is a smaller form of staging that can be fitted anywhere inside or around the outside of your greenhouse. Make sure that your shelving is deep enough to be effective and that there is enough space for a seed tray to sit on it. It is worth considering some benching, which is basically staging that can be stored when it is not in use. Fold it away and you have instant floor space for growing bags or pots. At the end of the growing season, bring it back to support overwintering crops.

Staging is easy to erect and vital for maximising floor space. Ready-made staging may be included in the price of a greenhouse, or can be bought separately. It is made from wood or aluminium and raises plants towards the light, ensuring healthy growth. It can be slatted, solid, or mesh. Always buy staging with a second level just above the ground. This uses space effectively and is ideal for overwintering plants that need protection from the cold.

ABOVE **The inside of a greenhouse**

ABOVE **Two-storey aluminium staging**

PREPARING THE GREENHOUSE

The organic principle of maintaining a healthy soil lends itself well to greenhouse culture. In an organic greenhouse, it should not be necessary to dig out the soil in the beds and replace it every year, as pests and diseases can be kept at bay following the advice in this book.

If you are going organic in your greenhouse for the first time, dig out the soil from the beds in autumn to a depth of around 12in (30cm). Break up the bottom with a fork, and replace it with well-rotted, friable, organic compost. In spring, add a top dressing of fresh compost and another application of blood, fish and bonemeal. Applying seaweed meal at this time will guard against potash shortage.

VENTILATION

Good ventilation is vital for plant health and it is an important part of controlling the temperature inside your greenhouse. You should be able to open the vents in your greenhouse easily, but automatic ones are inexpensive and simple to install. They open when the temperature rises to ventilate the greenhouse as necessary.

In cold, dull weather, poor ventilation can lead to humid, stale air, and various plant diseases such as moulds and rots thrive in such conditions. In sunny weather, temperatures will quickly rise to very high levels unless air can circulate. In the summer, temperatures inside the greenhouse can soar rapidly, so the door will need to be opened as well. Make sure your greenhouse has removable side panels for additional ventilation.

ABOVE **Moss and algae on the roof of a greenhouse show the effects of insufficient ventilation**

SHADING

Light is one of the most important factors of plant growth, and you should make sure that as much as possible is let in. On the other hand, plants can be actually scorched by the sun, so it pays to invest in some sort of shading. Specially formulated shading paint is available from home improvement centres. It is mixed like whitewash and it can be applied in spring and wiped off in autumn. Shading panels are available for some greenhouses, and are easy to clip into place on the inside of the glass or plastic. Shading fabrics such as plastic netting are another option. Internal or external roller blinds that can be adjusted as required are the best, but also the most expensive option.

CLEANING

It is a good idea to clean out your greenhouse thoroughly at least once a year. Dirty pots and seed trays can encourage pests and diseases. Late autumn or early winter is usually the most convenient time for this. Empty the greenhouse completely, then scrub down the inside of the glass, the frame, staging, shelves and floor using warm water, detergent and a soft brush. Scrape off any moss or algae. Scrub all the outside glass using clean water with a little garden disinfectant added, and then rinse well using a strong jet of water from a hose. Leave the door and the ventilators open and allow everything to dry thoroughly before returning the plants.

At the same time, sort out your pots. Discard any old and cracked ones, and keep any that are good enough to be re-used. Scrub them thoroughly with a nailbrush, using hot water to which a little washing-up liquid has been added. Sterilize all your pots once a year by scrubbing them in hot water with some garden disinfectant added. Allow them to dry and then stack them neatly according to size.

COLD FRAMES

Cold frames are small, low, semi-permanent structures with a sloping glazed top and glazed sides that protect plants during winter. They do not keep out much cold, but they will prevent plants from becoming waterlogged. For extra insulation, cover the frame with a blanket or a piece of carpet at night and insulate the sides with sheets of polystyrene, which can be cut to size using a knife.

Cold frames are almost airtight, so regular ventilation is important, and they should always be ventilated a little, both day and night. If cold frames are closed, condensation and dampness will build up, creating the conditions in which fungal diseases thrive. In mild or sunny weather, the glass roof or 'light' should be propped open every morning to prevent heat from the sun building up inside. Wide variations in the temperature can stress plants, making the foliage discolour and leaving them vulnerable to pests. Water plants well to maintain humidity in the frame when it is closed at night, and help to prevent pest infestation. Do not put too many plants into your frame or they will shade each other, leading to weak, leggy growth that will not withstand conditions in open ground.

The frame you choose must be deep enough to accommodate the range of plants you wish to grow, and it should let in plenty of light. Various designs are available in timber, metal and plastic, but modern cold frames usually have steel or aluminium frames and glass all round. The glass roof or 'light' is either hinged or designed to slide back. There are also solid-sided frames that retain more heat, but will not let in as much light. If light is a priority, choose a glass-to-ground frame.

A COLD FRAME

Glass roof or 'light'

Wooden frame

ABOVE **A cold frame can be used to acclimatize greenhouse-raised plants to outside conditions**

Before transferring greenhouse-raised crops to open ground, acclimatize them gradually in a cold frame. Bring greenhouse seedlings outside a week or so before you intend to plant them out and put them into a closed cold frame. Leave the frame closed for 24 hours. On the second day, open the top slightly and close it again at night. Gradually increase the width of the opening during the day but keep it almost closed at night. When the top is removed completely during the day, start opening the frame more at night. When the top is left off completely both day and night, the plants will be fully acclimatized and ready to plant in the open ground.

If you heat your cold frame, it can be used in exactly the same way as a greenhouse to produce plenty of seedlings and to grow fruits to maturity over a much extended season. It can also be used to harden off plants so they can be kept growing smoothly – the best way to ensure success. Small paraffin cold frame heaters are extremely economical to run.

ABOVE **A small paraffin cold frame heater**

CLOCHES AND TUNNELS

A cloche is a low, portable transparent cover used to warm up and dry out an area of ground before sowing or planting. Cloches are made from glass or plastic, though glass is rarely used now. Plastic cloches need replacing every three years or so. Buy a cloche that is convenient to use, allowing easy access to plants for weeding, general maintenance and harvesting, and that is easy to move.

Small tent cloches 12–18in (30–45cm) wide are used to start off seedlings or young plants. They look like an upturned 'V' and the plants will soon outgrow them. Tunnel or barn cloches are higher and wider at the top, so they are a better shape for more mature plants. If you have a large area of fruit to cover, a tunnel cloche is probably the best choice.

A cloche made from horticultural fleece is a good way to protect tender fruits from the winter cold. The polypropylene fleece is stabilised against ultra-violet light, and lets in air, light and moisture. Plants grow well underneath it, and it can lie on top of plants without harming them. Plants are less likely to suffer from wind damage, that can be a risk if you use plastic film. Make a fleece cloche by stapling a suitably-sized piece of the material between two wooden laths of the appropriate length. Place the fleece over the plants and hold it in place by burying the laths in the surrounding soil, or anchoring them with bricks. The cloche can remain in position over the plants until they mature.

A polythene film tunnel is a good and cheap alternative to a cloche. It is made from polythene sheeting stretched over wire hoops and secured with string or wires. The tunnel is ventilated by leaving the ends open or rolling up the sides. Polythene retains heat and transmits light well, but it will need to be replaced as it becomes yellow or torn. It can easily be dismantled for storage or moving to another part of the garden.

POLYTUNNELS

Walk-in polytunnels can be an excellent aid to growing fruit. The warmth and the humidity they offer are ideal for growing many types of fruits. Polytunnels come in a variety of sizes, and are also excellent for housing and propagating crops until they are ready to plant outside. On the minus side, these conditions can encourage fungus diseases such as moulds and rots, as well as pests like red spider mite, whitefly and slugs. It is not feasible to heat a polytunnel, and the plastic film will need to be replaced after about three years.

Polytunnels are made up of metal hoops attached at the top to a metal ridge pole with a wooden door frame at each end. The hoops are covered with plastic film sheet. Polytunnels are more airtight than greenhouses and retain heat accordingly. In hot weather, extra ventilation can be provided by cutting out small, low level vents along the sides of the tunnel. These can be taped back in winter.

Buy the biggest polytunnel you can afford and for which you have room. The larger the tunnel, the better the value. A polytunnel is much cheaper and easier to erect than a greenhouse, but bear in mind that the ridge should run from west to east so that the longest side gets the sun all day. A wide tunnel will give more working space from the sides, and ventilation is better. Do not site it in heavy shade. Polytunnels are relatively easy to move to another site in order to avoid pest and disease build up in the soil.

ABOVE **A large commercial polytunnel works on exactly the same principle as a the smaller ones used in gardens**

GREENHOUSE PESTS AND DISEASES

The closed atmosphere of the greenhouse can spread pests and diseases. Ventilation is essential, but when the ventilators or door are left open, pests find their way in. Insects can be controlled organically by encouraging natural predators such as ladybirds, lacewings, hoverflies, centipedes and black beetles. One way to combat pests is to introduce predators and parasites bought by mail order to the greenhouse early in the season. The larvae of the ladybird *Cryptolaemus montrouzieri* are good for mealy bugs, the parasitic midge *Aphididoletes aphidmyza* controls aphids, and the parasitic wasp *Encarsia Formosa* disposes of whitefly. Various natural remedies are available to discourage caterpillars.

Plant diseases are at their worst in early spring, autumn and winter when light is low and the air is cold and damp. Prevention is better than cure, so keep your greenhouse clean and tidy and sweep up dead or damaged material. Ventilate well to maintain air circulation around plants and discourage diseases that thrive in increased heat and humidity. In winter, water only when absolutely necessary. Sow seed later in the spring to prevent damping off.

ABOVE **Caterpillar on a leaf**
BELOW LEFT **Damaged grape vine leaf**

COMMON GREENHOUSE PROBLEMS

Pests	Diseases
Ants	Grey mould
Birds	Neck rot
Caterpillars	Powdery mildew
Mice	Root rot
Greenfly	Damping off
Red spider mite	(in seedlings)
Scale insect	
Slugs and snails	
Vine weevil	
Whitefly	
Woodlice	

CHAPTER 3

Buying fruit trees, bushes and canes

Cultivating fruit needs careful planning. Buy trees, bushes or canes from a specialist nursery. Young trees will establish quickly and crop earlier than older ones. Bare-rooted trees and bushes are usually cheaper and better quality than container-grown specimens. Plant them in winter when they are dormant or heel them in and set them in permanent position later. Choose varieties that are self-fertile, or will pollinate each other and remember that taste and texture are important. A specialist grower will be able to advise on the most suitable rootstock. Cordons, fans and espaliers are ideal for walls and fences. Trees are long-term investments: they may not crop for a few years. In most countries fruit is covered by a Government health scheme, so make sure they are certified free from disease.

ABOVE **Selection of fruit trees at a nursery**

ROOTSTOCKS

A rootstock is a selected root system on to which a variety is grafted to control the rate of growth and size of the mature tree. Some rootstocks have a dwarfing effect; apricots, for example, can be kept small by choosing the rootstock 'Pixy'. Grafting means joining a shoot or bud (the scion) of one plant to the stem and root system of another. The grafted variety dictates the type of fruit produced. Plant with the grafting point 4in (10cm) above the soil to prevent the variety from rooting.

BARE-ROOTED CHOICES

A one-year-old maiden is an untrained tree with no laterals. It must be pruned for about three years to produce a good framework of branches. A two-year old tree is partly trained, but training must be continued. Three to four-year old trees will be trained, but must be pruned to maintain a balance between growth and fruitfulness. A tree aged four or more is generally considered to be too old for training, and will be difficult and slow to establish.

ABOVE **Grafted union between rootstock and scion**

ROOTSTOCKS
M27: extremely dwarfing
Height of mature tree 5–6ft (1.5–1.8m).

M9: very dwarfing
Height of mature tree 10–12ft (3–3.6m)

M26: semi-dwarfing
Height of mature tree 14–18ft (4.2–5.4m)

MM111 and M2: vigorous
Height of mature tree 18–25ft (5.4–7.5m)

TREE SHAPES

There are many different sizes and shapes of tree you can choose from, according to the size of your garden and where you plan to grow it. This guide should help you to decide.

Standard trees are grown on vigorous or semi-vigorous rootstocks and make fine specimen trees, but are suitable only for large spaces and when top fruit is required. They are difficult to prune and pick because of their height, 15–25ft (4.5–7.5m).

BUSH

Bush is a popular shape because it soon comes into fruit and maintenance is easy. Bush trees are shorter than standards and have an open centre. The final size depends on the rootstock chosen.

PYRAMID

Pyramid is similar to bush, but the central leader is maintained to give a conical shape. It needs careful pruning in summer and is suitable for a container because it is easy to prune and pick. A dwarf pyramid can grow to 7ft (2.1m).

ABOVE **Apple tree in blossom**

CORDON

ESPALIER

Cordons are single-stemmed trees that usually reach a height of around 6ft (1.8m). They are planted at 45° and supported on a fence or post and wires. Several varieties can be grown in a restricted space.

Espalier is an attractive wall feature, but it takes up more space than a cordon. Branches emerge horizontally from the stem at intervals of about 18in (45cm). Buy them ready-trained if possible. Espaliers can reach 8ft (2.4m).

Fan shapes are decorative when planted against a wall, but need careful training. They are usually pruned so two opposing shoots from the main stem form the 'fan'. They are used more widely for cherries, plums and peaches than for apples, and reach about 6ft (1.8m).

FAN

Step-over (below) is a single-tier espalier with one branch on each side of the main stem. It can be used as an edging for a bed or border, or along paths. An extremely dwarfing rootstock is used so it only grows to about 12in (30cm).

STEP-OVER

POLLINATION

This is the transfer of pollen from the male part (anther) of the flower to the female part (stigma), resulting in fertilization followed by fruit set. Most soft fruits and some fruit trees are self-fertile, which means they are fertilized by their own pollen and can be grown singly. Self-sterile cultivars must be cross-pollinated by a cultivar of the same fruit. Choose self-fertile trees, or two that will pollinate each other. Apples, pears, cherries and some plums are not reliably self-fertile, so plant them close to one or more cultivars of the same fruit and insects will cross-pollinate them. 'Triploids' must be grown in threes. Greenhouse and early-flowering plants need hand-pollinating because there will be few insects about. Dab the centre of each flower gently with a soft brush, daily when the weather is warm and dry and the flowers are fully open.

Varieties of apples, pears, plums, cherries, damsons and gages are divided according to when the flowers open and are ready to be pollinated. Trees in the same pollination group will cross-pollinate because they are in flower at the same time. The groups are:

1 Early flowering
2 Mid-season flowering
3 Mid season/late flowering
4 Mid season/late flowering triploid
5 Late flowering
6 Late flowering triploid needing two pollination partners

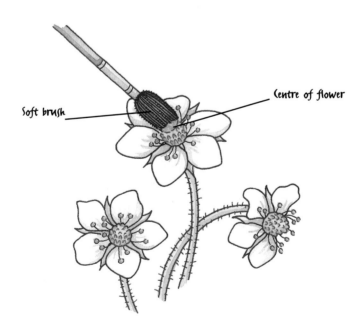

ABOVE **Hand-pollinating a strawberry flower**

48

COMPANION PLANTING IN THE GARDEN

Many types of fruit are self-fertile, but others must be cross-pollinated. Some fruits and nuts are pollinated by wind, others by bees and insects. Fruit flowers can be hand-pollinated (see illustration opposite), but this is a tedious and lengthy task so it is far better to encourage pollination by insects.

Plant flowers that provide nectar for bees, hoverflies and other beneficial insects, to attract them to the garden. Grow ground-cover plants as a habitat for ground beetles. Herbs are long-flowering and benefit various pollinators and predators. The smell of alliums such as garlic and chives deters many pests, and their flowers attract beneficial insects.

SUGGESTED FLOWERS AND HERBS
Poached egg plant *Limnanthes douglassii*
Pot marigold *Calendula officinalis*
French marigold *Tagetes patula*
Convolvulus tricolor 'Blue Flash'
California bluebell *Phacelia campanularia*
Evening primrose *Oenothera biennis*
Aster *Aster turbinellus*

Various spring-flowering plants
Rosemary *Rosmarinus officinalis*
Thyme *Thymus vulgare*
Sage *Salvia officinalis*
Southernwood *Artemisia abrotanum*
Lavender *Lavandula angustifolia*
Angelica *Angelica archangelica*
Borage *Borago officinalis*

ABOVE **Rosemary**

ABOVE **Lavender**

ABOVE **Pot marigold**

GENERAL PRUNING

Pruning has two main purposes: to remove damaged, diseased and unproductive growth and to channel energy into fruit production. It is also used to reduce the size of a plant that has become too large. When pruning, always take into account the vigour of the tree and its individual shoots. Careful pruning maintains an open structure which lets the sun reach the fruit. During the first four years of the life of a tree, pruning is done to produce a good shape and a balanced framework. Selecting and tying in shoots to create a particular shape is called training. Young plants can be given specific shapes, such as espalier or fan, by combining pruning and training. Follow-up pruning of established plants helps to maintain the health and shape of the plant, and to ensure a satisfactory yield.

ABOVE **A large apple tree growing in a garden**

WHEN AND HOW TO PRUNE

A fruit tree aged four or more is considered established, and should be pruned every year. Winter pruning is usual for all untrained quince, pear and apple trees, vines, and for currants, gooseberries and blueberries. Untrained stone fruit trees such as plum and cherry are pruned in spring when young, or in summer if established. Summer pruning is essential for trained fruit forms, grape vines, gooseberries and currants, to concentrate the plants' energies into fruit production. Many tender fruits are pruned directly after fruiting.

Fruit trees are divided into two main groups: spur-bearing and tip-bearing. Spur bearers bear most of their fruit on older wood, which must be retained. Cut back the leading shoots on each branch, cutting the strong ones by a quarter and weaker ones by half. Prune the strong side shoots to six buds and any weaker ones to four. To improve fruit quality thin overcrowded spurs, removing about a third of the weakest shoots to create an open spur. Tip bearers produce fruit on year-old wood, so remove a third of the older wood and trim any long, new shoots. Do not prune the shorter maiden shoots that have fruit buds at their tips.

Prune vigorous growth lightly and weak growth more severely, checking that the weakness is not caused by disease. Prune just above a healthy bud, making a clean cut. Cut branches or shoots back to their original points. Take care to leave the branch collar intact so the tree will be less susceptible to disease.

ABOVE **Pruning a newly-planted whitecurrant**

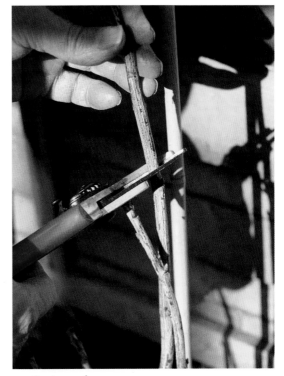

ABOVE **Pruning a redcurrant**

TRAINING TREES

Trained trees may bear fruit for more than twenty years, so they need a durable support structure. This structure can take the form of horizontal wires across a fence or a wall, or wires that run horizontally between posts. Use heavy-duty wire pulled taut between straining bolts. Fix vine eyes to the wall or fence posts to support the wires. Use the longest ones possible to allow the air to circulate behind the trees and reduce the possibility of disease. Fix the first wire 6–30in (15–75cm) off the ground and the other wires 18–24in (45–60cm) apart, depending on the fruit. Train step-overs on a single wire fixed 12in (30cm) above the ground.

A POST AND WIRES SUPPORT

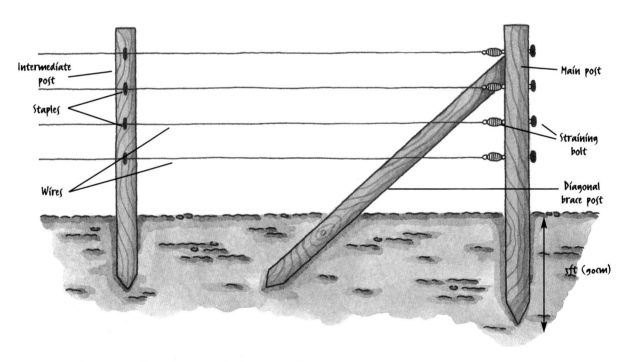

ABOVE **Make sure you use heavy-duty wires, and sink the posts well into the ground for stability**

CORDONS

Construct a post and wire support or string wires horizontally to a wall at 24in (60cm) intervals. Tie canes to the wires so the plant stems do not rub against them, then plant the cordons 30in (75cm) apart, in the middle of the angled wires. Cut the leading shoot back to two-thirds of the year's growth and the side shoots to 3in (7.5cm), cutting to a downward-facing bud. During the first summer, prune back the side shoots to 3in (7.5cm) and the secondary shoots to 1in (2.5cm). In the second winter, prune the leading shoot to two thirds of the year's growth. Prune in the same way every summer until it reaches the top of the cane, then prune the leading shoot in summer to 3in (7.5cm) and the side shoots to 1in (2.5cm).

ESPALIERS

Construct a post and wire support, or string three wires horizontally to a wall. Plant the tree and prune to 2in (5cm) above the first wire, leaving three good buds. In spring, train the side shoots to the angled canes. In summer, prune the branches on the leading shoot to 3in (7.5cm). In winter, tie two branches to the lower wire and prune the leading shoot to 2in (5cm) above the second wire. In the second summer, prune the side shoots to 3in (7.5cm) and the secondary shoots to 1in (2.5cm). In the third summer, prune and train the second tier of branches as you did the first. Repeat the process every summer until you reach the required height. Train two buds for the final tier then prune each arm every summer as for cordons.

ABOVE **An espaliered loganberry is still an attractive feature in autumn**

FANS

In the first year, choose two healthy laterals of a feathered maiden tree, 12in (30cm) above soil level. Cut off the leader above the top lateral. Prune each lateral to 15in (37.5cm) to encourage sub-laterals to grow, and tie to canes attached at 40° to the wires. Cut back other laterals to one bud. In summer, select two evenly-spaced shoots from the upper side of each branch and one from below to form the 'ribs', and tie to canes set at 30°. Remove any badly-positioned shoots and select one to continue the main laterals. Pinch back the others to one leaf. In the second year before bud burst, cut back extension growth on the main arms by a quarter, to a strong bud. In early summer, tie in selected shoots to fill the framework, adding canes as necessary. Remove shoots that are weak, over-vigorous, or facing inwards. In early spring of the third year, shorten new ribs by a quarter and select further shoots to complete the main ribs. Remove any shoots growing the wrong way, and thin side shoots growing in line with the fan shape to 4–6in (10–15cm) apart. As the branches fill out, prune back any overlapping shoots to 4–6 leaves. Remove any upright growth above the top support wire. Thereafter, prune to avoid overcrowding.

CENTRAL-LEADER STANDARD TREES

Prune young feathered trees over two or three years to form a central-leader standard with about 6ft (1.8m) of clear stem. The first spring after planting, cut back flush with the main stem the laterals on the lowest third of the tree, and by half those on the central third. From the top third, remove any competing or weak leaders. In the second and third years, prune in spring as before. Remove the lowest laterals, cut back by half those on the central third of the tree, and leave the top third unpruned. Repeat in late autumn or early winter.

FEATHERED TREE

Remove any crossing or congested shoots. Cut out any badly positioned, spindly or small laterals to give a well-balanced framework.

TREE FRUITS/TOP FRUITS

This group of large forms comprises pome fruits with a pip-containing core, such as apples, pears and quinces, and stone fruits with a hard, central stone, such as cherries and apricots. Some fruit, including figs, mulberries and persimmons fit into neither category.

ABOVE **A newly-planted apple tree**

MAYPOLING

To support heavily-laden branches, tie a pole or stake to the main trunk of the tree. Attach several pieces of rope or thick string to the pole, then tie each of the free ends to a branch that needs support. This produces a 'maypole' effect. Pot-grown plants can be supported in the same way using a central cane and lengths of plastic wire.

A MAYPOLED TREE

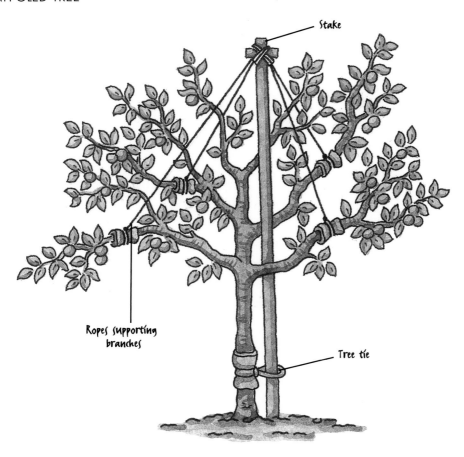

Stake

Ropes supporting branches

Tree tie

ABOVE **Maypoling is an ideal way to support the heavily-laden branches of fruit trees**

GUYOT SYSTEM

This system is usually used to train outdoor grape vines. The single Guyot form has one fruit-carrying arm, and the double Guyot (the most popular form) has two. Every year, let three main stems or rods develop. Retain two for fruiting, and cut the third back. Train the two selected rods close to the ground.

THE DOUBLE GUYOT SYSTEM

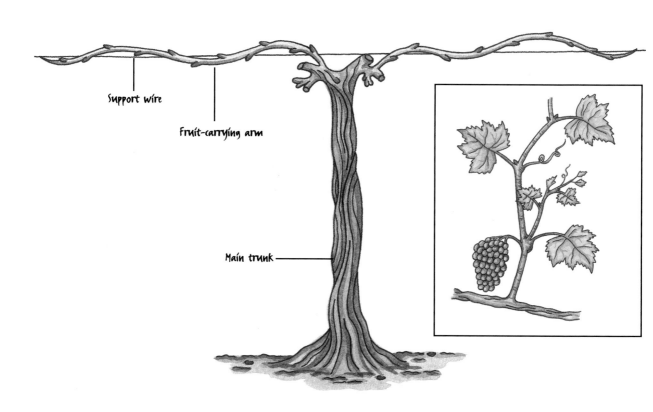

Support wire

Fruit-carrying arm

Main trunk

ABOVE **The Guyot system is widely used for training outdoor grape vines**
INSET **Vine leaves and grapes from the fruit-carring arm**

ABOVE **Gooseberry bushes have beautiful foliage and look attractive in the border even before they fruit**

SOFT FRUITS

Unlike most tree or top fruits, soft fruits are self-fertile, so you can grow a single plant and it will bear a crop. Soft fruits need less space than most tree fruits and pruning is usually easier. They bear fruit quite soon after planting, although their fruit producing life-span is shorter.

Many types of soft fruit, such as climbing grapes and kiwi fruits, need extra support because their stems are weak. The tall, flexible canes of blackberries and raspberries can easily be damaged by the wind. Bush fruits like currants and gooseberries do not usually need support, but if they are cultivated as cordons the single tall shoot is tied to canes and wires. Training a free-standing bush promotes better cropping and makes it easier to prune and maintain. Make sure that you cut out some of the shoots at an early stage of growth to prevent overcrowding, and select the rest carefully so the plant has a fairly hollow central area.

Soft fruits need to be protected from birds, but netting is adequate if you only have one plant. If you want to grow larger quantities of soft fruit, you might consider building a special fruit cage.

ABOVE **Blackberry canes bear fruit in the second year after planting**

TYPES OF SOFT FRUIT

Bedding varieties: Hardy, non-woody plants that bear fruit within a year if planted in late summer, for example strawberries.

Bush varieties: Hardy, woody plants with spreading, fruit-bearing branches that are not all cut away after cropping, for example gooseberry, blackcurrant, red and white currant.

Cane varieties: Hardy, woody plants with long, slender shoots that bear fruit in the second year after planting, for example raspberry and blackberry.

Tender varieties: Frost-sensitive or warmth-loving plants which must be grown in a greenhouse in cooler climates, for example Cape gooseberry, grape, kiwi fruit, melon.

FRUIT PROPAGATION

Alpine strawberries, avocado pear, melon and Cape gooseberry are usually grown from seed, and tropical cultivars such as passion fruit, mango and papaya, can also be raised in this way. Several tender fruits and some nuts may be grown from seed, but hardy fruits seldom come true. Vines, figs and many soft fruits are propagated by cuttings, while some fruits produce runners, layers, or suckers. Tree fruits including apple, pear, plum, peach and cherry are usually propagated by grafting. Chip-budding and T-budding will produce a new tree from a single bud.

SEED

This can be collected for use the following spring. Pick fleshy fruit, such as melon, when it is ripe or slightly over-ripe. Remove the seed, wash thoroughly, dry and store in an airtight container. Before planting, test its viability by placing a few between two pieces of moist kitchen or blotting paper. Leave for a couple of weeks. If they have not sprouted by then it is unlikely that they will. In cooler climates, grow seed from a specialist supplier in a greenhouse.

ABOVE **Seed can be collected from honeydew melons and dried ready to grow new plants**

ABOVE **A lemon seedling (left) and a pineapple top (right)**

59

GRAFTING

This is widely used to produce uniform plants. For the rootstock, choose an established plant with a stem at least ½in (12mm) thick.

CLEFT GRAFTING

This method allows a much smaller scion to be grafted to a larger rootstock. It is done in late winter when the rootstock and scion are both dormant. It works well on mangos and avocados. Choose seeds from the fruit of trees that grow well in your area. Cleft grafting can also be used to add a branch to an existing tree, or to replace one that has broken off.

METHOD

1 Plant the seed in plastic tree bags and allow each stem to grow for seven or eight months.

2 Select and cut vigorous 6in (15cm) shoots of the current season's ripened wood.

3 Using a very sharp knife, make two sloping cuts 1.5in (3.5cm) long at the bottom of each budstick.

4 Select a scion the same thickness as the stem of the rootstock. Cut off the soft tip and remove all the leaves.

5 Cut off the rootstock 12in (30cm) above soil level. Make a straight cut 1in (2.5cm) deep in the top.

6 Push the scion into the straight cut of the rootstock, leaving ¼in (6mm) of the cut scion outside. Join the two using clear plastic tape and leave until the scion begins to grow, removing any buds that grow beneath the graft.

CHIP-BUDDING

This reliable method is the one most widely used for fruit trees. In mid-summer, a bud (chip) is removed from the budstick (scion) and grafted to a suitable rootstock, from which a similar-sized chip of ripe wood has been removed.

METHOD

1 Choose a vigorous shoot of the current season's ripened wood. Cut off the soft tip and remove leaves to leave a clear length of stem.

2 Cut ¼in (6mm) deep and ¾in (18mm) below a bud, keeping the knife at a 45° angle.

3 Place the knife 1.5in (4cm) above the first cut and slice down behind the bud to meet it. Remove the chip, holding it by the bud.

4 Remove the shoots and leaves from the bottom 12in (30cm) of the rootstock stem. Make a similar cut in it, and remove the sliver to expose the cambium layer.

5 Position the bud chip and rootstock so the cambium layers touch. Bind with clear plastic tape, and leave in place for a few weeks.

6 The following winter, remove the stem above the grafted bud using an angled cut. In spring, a healthy, new shoot will develop from the bud.

RIGHT **Peaches can be propagated by chip-budding**

T-BUDDING

This is similar to chip-budding, but the bud is inserted in a T-shaped cut in the rootstock. It is effective when the rootstock and budstock are different sizes. It is done in summer, preferably in cool, showery weather, when the rootstock is still growing vigorously but the wood has hardened slightly, and the scion buds at the base of the leaf stems are mature.

METHOD

1 Choose a ripened shoot from the current season's growth and remove the leaves.

2 Slice underneath a bud to remove it, but leave a strip of bark that extends about 1in (2.5cm) above and below it. Pull away the woody bits from behind the bud.

3 Make a T-shaped cut about 1–1½in (2.5–4cm) high and ½in (12mm) wide in the rootstock, 6–12in (15–30cm) above soil level. Prise open the flaps of the bark.

4 Insert the bud behind the flaps. Trim away the surplus top, making sure it is level with the horizontal cut on the rootstock. Secure the bud using clear tape.

5 When the shoot develops the next spring, cut off the rootstock growth above the bud.

WHIP-AND-TONGUE GRAFTING

This method is most successful for pome fruits including apples, pears and quinces. It is the primary method of propagating pecan nursery stock in the US. It is also used to propagate grapes. Whip grafting works best when there is high humidity, so avoid it in dry areas. When buds begin to grow on the scion, select the best shoot to form a maiden whip tree.

METHOD

1 In mid-winter, cut six or seven 9in (23cm) lengths of vigorous hardwood shoots, just above a bud, from the scion tree. Group them, and heel them into well-drained soil in a sheltered spot, with the tops 2–3in (5–7.5cm) above soil level.

2 In early spring, cut off the top of each rootstock about 8–10in (20–25cm) above soil level. Trim off any shoots on the rootstock using a sharp knife.

3 Make a 1½in (4cm) slanting cut on the rootstock to expose the cambium layer. Make a further ½in (12mm) slit about a third of the way down the cambium layer to produce a 'tongue'.

4 Dig up the scions, cut off any soft tip growth and trim to three or four buds.

5 Working on one scion at a time, cut off a piece of bark behind a bud about 2in (5cm) from the bottom. Cut the cambium layer to match the tongue in the rootstock.

6 Slip the rootstock and scion together so the tongues join. Bind together with clear plastic tape and leave until a callus has formed around the graft union.

LEFT **Pears are often propagated by whip-and-tongue grafting**

SOFT FRUIT BUSH PROPAGATION

For red and white currants and gooseberries, take 12–15in (30–37.5cm) cuttings from clean, vigorous, well-ripened shoots of the current season's growth in mid-autumn. Trim off the leaves and soft tip and remove the lower buds, leaving four to five top buds. Make a narrow trench 6in (15cm) deep and insert the cuttings, firming the soil around them. The following autumn, lift the new, rooted plants carefully and transplant to their growing position.

For blackcurrants, take 8–10in (20–25cm) hardwood cuttings in autumn leaving all the buds intact. Bury in the ground with just two buds showing. Dig up for transplanting the following autumn, by which time they should have 3–4 good stems.

Propagate blackberries, loganberries and tayberries by tip layering. In summer, poke the growing tip of a stem down into the soil so it is buried about 4–5in (10–12.5cm) deep. In autumn or early winter sever the new plant, which will have formed roots, from the parent plant. Either pot up for planting later, or set out in its planting position.

For blueberries, guavas and pomegranates, take 4–6in (10–15cm) softwood cuttings in mid-summer. Dip the cuttings in rooting powder and insert in an acidic peat/sand rooting medium. Place in a heated propagator until they have rooted. Transplant into a larger pot and harden off in a shaded cloche or cold frame before planting outside.

ABOVE **Red and white currant bushes**

ABOVE **Taking blackcurrant cuttings**

ABOVE **Blackcurrant cuttings with two buds showing**

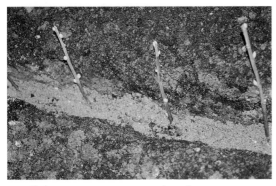

ABOVE **Blackcurrant cuttings in a prepared trench**

Plants like strawberries have horizontal creeping stems or runners that root where they come into contact with the ground. Lift them with a trowel and either pot up for future use, or plant in their permanent growing positions.

Cane fruit including raspberries, figs, filberts and cobnuts produce suckers. Lift and sever these in the autumn when the plants are dormant, and transplant to their permanent growing positions.

Blackberries can also be propagated by leaf-bud cuttings. Take strong, healthy 12in (30cm) shoots with plenty of buds from the current season's growth. Make a $\frac{1}{2}$in (12mm) cut above a bud and slice down to remove it, plus about 1in (2.5cm) of stem with a leaf attached. Plant in pots with the stem portions at an angle and the growth buds just above the ground. Water and place in a cold frame until rooted.

ABOVE **Strawberries have runners that creep horizontally along the ground and root to form new plants**

ROUTINE MAINTENANCE

Using manure or compost, mulch newly planted trees in spring. When they reach flowering size, apply an organic fertilizer in early spring, but do not overfeed as this could result in soft, disease-prone growth. Mulch specimen trees planted in lawns with the mowings when the grass is cut. This will return nutrients to the soil and help to avoid potassium deficiency. For soft fruits, apply organic surface mulches such as straw, coconut fibre or farmyard manure in spring to suppress weeds and help to retain moisture. Apply an organic fertilizer as required. Dig in some well-rotted manure before planting strawberries. Water all fruits as necessary. Some fruits must be thinned to obtain crops of a good size and quality. Remove any disfigured or unhealthy fruit and thin the rest to 2–3in (5–7.5cm) apart.

In winter, birds damage fruit buds by feeding on the centre of them. Protect them by placing nets over the trees or bushes. Ripening fruit should also be protected from birds. Small areas can be covered with netting, but for larger areas it is better to erect a fruit cage.

Protect early-flowering fruit crops from spring frosts. Strawberries can be damaged by late spring frosts when they are in flower, so cover them with straw, hessian, fleece, or polythene when frost is forecast. Cover wall fruits with thick netting, hessian or fleece at night. Protect bush fruits and small trees in the same way.

ABOVE **A small orange tree growing in a galvanized container**

ABOVE **A mature apple tree bearing a good crop of fruit**

ABOVE **Netting draped over canes is used to protect whitecurrants**

CHAPTER 4

Growing fruit

This chapter looks at the general requirements for successful fruit growing. Fruit will grow in most types of soil, as long as it is reasonably well-drained. With the right preparation, you will be able to enjoy a good variety of home-grown produce. The A–Z Directory of plants that follows contains alphabetical listings of various fruit and their specific growing requirements. There is also a section on the most useful companion plants for your crops. These are an integral part of organic gardening, and can be used in many ways to help to create the ideal growing conditions for fruit in your garden.

ABOVE **Flowering blackberry bush**

SOIL REQUIREMENTS

Successful gardening requires rich, fertile soil. For the best results, fruit should be grown in soil that is friable, rich and moist. As a general guide, the larger the plant the greater the depth of soil needed. For tree, bush and cane fruits, soil depth should be at least 18in (45cm) and for strawberries at least 12in (30cm).

All soil contains reserves of plant food, which are replenished when plants die and rot down. Growing plants take part of their food from the soil, but the ideal balance is easily upset. Continuous cultivation and harvesting, plus the effect of rain which can leach essential nutrients from the soil, means that its reserves may be depleted more rapidly than they can be replaced naturally. In time, this will cause a shortage of some essential nutrients and your plants will fail to thrive.

To maintain or increase the fertility of your soil, major plant foods and trace elements must be returned at regular intervals. This can be done quite easily with manures and fertilizers. Organic fertilizers are simple to use and are completely safe and natural. They do not harm the soil and the effects usually last far longer than those of their chemical counterparts.

ABOVE **Heavy clay soil**

IDENTIFYING SOIL TYPE

Some plants will have more specific soil requirements, so it is good policy to determine the type of soil you have from the outset.

Clay soil sticks together in lumps or bakes hard in the sun and cracks deeply. It is a 'cold' soil that takes a long time to warm up in spring, so fruit picking is later. It is normally well supplied with plant foods, and can become workable, fertile soil if plenty of bulky organic matter is added and drainage is improved.

Sandy soil is light, easy to work, warms up quickly in spring, and can be cultivated earlier than most soils. It is gritty, free-draining and does not lump together. It is poor in nutrients, which are easily lost, and needs large amounts of organic matter and extra fertilizer added.

Chalky soil is pale, free-draining and similar to sandy soil, but contains a lot of lime so is always alkaline. Alkaline soils can be deficient in manganese and iron, which can cause yellowing leaves and stunted growth. The topsoil is usually shallow, so it is unsuitable for plants with deep roots. Water and nutrients must be retained by adding organic material, which will also help to make the soil more acid.

ABOVE **Workable, loamy soil**

SOIL LAYERS

To get the best from your soil, you should make sure that you can recognize its two main layers:

Topsoil is the fertile upper layer of soil, which contains beneficial bacteria and organic matter. It is usually about 12in (30cm) deep, but on well-cultivated ground, the topsoil layer may be up to 24in (60cm) deep. In chalky areas, the topsoil may be as shallow as 2in (5cm).

Subsoil is the soil that is left after the topsoil has been removed. It may be hard and cracked. Subsoil is usually lighter in colour than topsoil, because it lacks organic matter and bacteria. It contains no humus and is largely without nutrients. When you are digging, take care never to bury topsoil under subsoil. It is best to remove and bag it for future use.

IDEAL SOIL

The ideal soil for producing high yields of good-quality fruit will be a mixture of sand and clay with a large amount of humus. It will be dark and rich in colour with a crumbly, medium-loam texture and well-drained subsoil. The soil should contain sufficient lime to counteract soil sourness, a substantial amount of humus, and adequate plant foods to produce maximum growth. There are many things you can do to improve the quality of your soil, but if it is really poor or the topsoil layer is too shallow, the only option may be to have a load of new topsoil delivered.

IMPROVING SOIL STRUCTURE

Tree, bush and cane fruits have a relatively long life, and good ground preparation is the secret of achieving good crops. Before planting anything, prepare the ground thoroughly by manuring and if necessary, liming. In autumn or early winter, spread bulky organic matter over the surface at a rate of about 10lb (4.5kg) per sq yd (sq m). Fork the layer of humus in before you start digging. This will improve crumb structure and will greatly increase the soil's capacity to hold nutrients and water.

Growing fruits do not need lime unless the soil is very acid. Test your soil with a pH testing kit (see page 71) and add lime if necessary to achieve the right pH reading. Use ground limestone rather than hydrated lime.

ABOVE **Incorporate plenty of bulky organic matter as you dig, to improve the crumb structure of the soil and greatly increase its capacity to hold nutrients and water.**

DRAINAGE

In winter, badly-drained soil is likely to become waterlogged. The water that has not drained away forces air from the soil, so the roots of plants will be drowned. Double digging (to a depth equivalent to two spades) can help to solve the problem, because it will break up the subsoil and allow water to pass through, but it will only be effective if there is somewhere for the water to flow to.

The signs of poor drainage include water that lies on the surface of the soil for several days, and soil that is greyish, bluish or mottled. Other indications include sparse vegetation and a lack of earthworms. The topsoil may be poor, for example, clay soil with little organic matter.

To combat poor drainage, fork in plenty of bulky organic material. This will encourage worm activity and absorb a great deal of water, helping to solve the problem. If the problem persists, the best solution is to dig trench drains or install a soakaway (see right) at the lowest point of your plot.

Dig trench drains about 12in (30cm) wide and 2–3ft (60–90cm) deep, on either side of a level site, or across the lower end of a slope. Fill the bottom end of the newly-dug trench with stones and clinkers before replacing the soil. This should ease the problem, as the trench will usually absorb the water and allow the soil to become more workable.

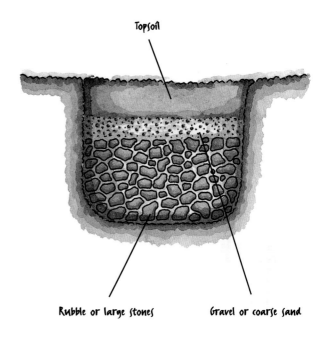

Topsoil

Rubble or large stones   Gravel or coarse sand

CONSTRUCTING A SOAKAWAY

1 Dig a hole at least 2ft (60cm) square and 3ft (90cm) deep at the lowest point in the garden.

2 Fill the hole to within 12in (30cm) of the top with rubble or large stones.

3 Cover the rubble or stones with a 6in (15cm) layer of gravel or coarse sand.

4 Finish with a 6in (15cm) layer of topsoil to ground level.

ABOVE **Dig the soil in late autumn or winter**

DIGGING YOUR SOIL

In late autumn to early winter, mark out the length and breadth of your plot. Place a cane in each of the four corners, and join them using lengths of garden twine or strong string. Remove any debris such as stones or pieces of wood, and cut down tall weeds and grass using a strimmer.

Dig the soil roughly, leaving it in fairly large lumps. Digging introduces air into the soil and encourages the biological activity necessary for soil fertility. The clods of earth that are produced will be broken down by the winter frosts, thus improving the texture. Digging also corrects any damage caused by heavy rain and footsteps walking over the plot, which over time impairs the crumb structure and drainage. Incorporate plenty of organic matter as you dig. In early spring the soil should be crumbly and workable, not sticky but just moist, and ready for you to dig it over again in preparation for planting. Do not dig your soil when it is very wet or the structure may be harmed.

If the soil in your garden is light, you will not need to dig it. Instead, mulch the soil with layers of well-rotted organic material to improve its fertility, then allow worm activity to incorporate it into the soil. Young plants can then be grown through the mulch.

Single digging

Dig each area separately to the depth of one spit – the length of your spade's blade. Do not try to dig all four areas at once: pace yourself. Dig over a period of a few days to prevent any strains or injuries. When digging, do not bring up any of the subsoil.

Double digging

This is done in a similar way to single digging but to twice the depth. Work from side to side of the plot as above, but this time dig to a depth of two spits and produce trenches about 18in (45cm) deep. Double-dig soil that is not free draining every three or four years, to encourage plants to form good root systems. It will also break up the compacted layer of soil that may have formed below the depth of digging.

Digging trenches

Working from one side of the plot to the other, dig out a single trench. Barrow the soil from this first trench to the far end of the plot, and use it to fill the last trench. Fork over the bottom of each trench as you work to break up the subsoil. As the soil is turned, fork in organic matter. Replace the soil from the second trench into the third trench, from the third trench into the fourth trench, and so on across the plots. Continue to the end of each plot or area, keeping the soil as level as possible. Finish by filling the last trench with the soil from the first.

ABOVE **pH soil-testing kit**

SOIL READINGS

The acidity or alkalinity of your soil depends on how much calcium it contains. Calcium levels are measured on the pH scale 0–14, and neutral soil has a reading of pH7. A simple testing kit from a garden centre or nursery will indicate an approximate pH value, which is precise enough as all plants possess some tolerance. Any soil below pH7 will be acid; any soil above will be alkaline. Most fruits grow best in a slightly acid soil, pH6–6.5. Soils below about pH6 will need lime.

ORGANIC FERTILIZERS

Organic fertilizers are ecologically sound and environmentally safe, and last far longer in the soil than chemical ones. They do not harm the soil, but benefit both the crops grown in it and the wildlife that live in it. They are available as powders, ground manure or pellets, which are the easiest to use. They are of either animal or vegetable origin, and supply plants with the nutrients they need over a period of time. Apply according to the instructions on the packet.

DRIED BLOOD
(12–13 per cent nitrogen)
This is a fast-acting fertilizer. Apply at the rate of 1–2oz per sq yd (25–55g per sq m). Water in well after each application, and either work it into the soil when growth is active, or mix it with water and apply it around the roots of the plants.

HOOF AND HORN
This valuable source of nitrogen is made from the ground sterilised hooves and horns of cattle. It is broken down by the bacteria in the soil over a long period of time, ensuring a steady supply of the element to the plants. Work hoof and horn into the soil 2–3 weeks before planting so it has time to work.

BONEMEAL
(30 per cent phosphates/1.5 per cent nitrogen)
This is an excellent dressing that is often used in seedbeds. Apply at the rate of 2–4oz per sq yd (55–114g per sq m). It is a good source of phosphate, which is released slowly, aiding seed germination, stimulating root and pod growth, and promoting the early ripening of fruits and roots. Always buy the steam-treated product as raw bonemeal may contain anthrax, and wear gloves when applying.

WOOD ASH
This is the main organic supply of potash, an important nutrient that counteracts soft growth, and helps in the formation of storage material. It acts quickly when applied to growing plants. Potash counterbalances the effect of excess nitrogen, and increases the resistance of plants to disease by helping them to withstand frost and other adverse weather conditions, such as drought. It can make wet soils stickier, so apply in spring when the soil is dry and hoe well in.

PELLETED POULTRY MANURE
This useful, quick-acting, general garden fertilizer contains a balance of nutrients, the highest of which is nitrogen. It has a strong smell, and can be used as a top-dressing for leafy plants, as well as a compost activator.

SEAWEED MEAL
This is a useful multi-purpose fertilizer made from dried and ground seaweed. It supplies trace elements and essential nutrients, and is an excellent activator for the compost heap. When applied to the soil at the rate of 3oz per sq yd (85g per sq m) it is a good source of potash.

BLOOD, FISH AND BONE
This useful, balanced general fertilizer is a mixture of dried blood, fish meal and ground bones. It releases nitrogen quickly and phosphate at a slower rate. It can be used as a pre-planting dressing and also as a compost activator.

COMFREY AND NETTLES
A great liquid fertilizer for most plants can be made by rotting down comfrey and nettle leaves in a bucket of water. Use diluted.

ABOVE **Comfrey**

ABOVE **Nettle: comfrey and nettle makes a good organic fertilizer**

ABOVE **Homemade mulch made from bark chippings**

MULCHES

A mulch is simply a layer of material that covers the soil. It can be inorganic, for example plastic or polythene, or organic, for example well-rotted manure. Mulching helps to keep the ground weed-free, reduces the effects of summer drought, and acts as an insulating blanket, protecting young or delicate roots from extremes of temperature. In winter, a layer of mulch reduces the risk of soil freezing around the roots of plants, and in summer it provides protection against the scorching sun. Mulching also protects soil from heavy rain. It should be spread to a depth of at least 4in (10cm) to be effective. Stone mulches are ideal for areas where drainage is necessary. Spread a layer of gravel to a thickness of 1–2in (2.5–5cm).

On the downside, mulching may encourage slugs and prevent light rain from reaching the soil. As organic mulches decay, they become an ideal place for weed seed germination.

ABOVE **An electric shredder is useful for making mulches and for shredding compost**

GREEN MANURE

This is a term applied to a crop that has been grown simply to put it back into the soil. To improve an area of soil, try putting it down to green manure for 6–12 months.

The most obvious uses of green manure are that it provides organic matter and increases biological activity. The roots of the plant break up the soil and improve drainage. An autumn sowing of green manure will help protect the soil over the winter, and when it is dug into the ground in spring, it will decay and release valuable nutrients for the following crop.

Sow the seed as directed on the packet and let the plants grow until the ground is needed again. Dig the plants into the soil and allow them to decay, then sow or plant the plot as usual. Choose a variety that is different from the crop you plan to sow next and the one you have just harvested. Make sure it will mature in the time available before you need the plot.

ABOVE **Clover is an ideal crop for green manuring**

PLANTS FOR GREEN MANURE
Nitrogen fixers
Alfalfa (lucerne) *Medicago sativa*
Tall perennial that must occupy land for a whole season.

Red Clover *Trifolium pratense*
Low-growing plant that should be dug in when the land is needed.

Winter tare *Vicia villosa*
Tall plant that produces large amounts of green matter over winter and should be dug in early spring.

Plants that do not fix nitrogen
Phacelia *Phacelia tanacetifolia*
Fast-growing plant that does not withstand cold and should be dug in about eight weeks after sowing.

Rye *Secale cereale*
Sow the perennial variety of this plant, which produces a useful amount of green material, and dig in during the spring.

Mustard *Sinapis alba*
This fast-growing plant produces plenty of green matter and suppresses weeds well. Dig in before it flowers.

Mustard is a member of the cabbage family, so it could harbour club-root.

THE COMPOST HEAP

Composting is the process via which organic material is broken down by micro-organisms, mainly bacteria and fungi. It is the ideal way of returning organic material to the soil. Good compost improves soil structure and fertility and provides plant foods for crops. It also increases worm activity and the water-holding capacity of the soil, and reduces the need for artificial fertilizers. In addition to composting material, the heap must have air, nitrogen, lime, water, heat and bacteria.

Garden centres and nurseries sell a wide variety of compost bins and containers, or you can make your own. Size will depend on the size of your garden, but the larger the receptacle the better the air circulation. Ideally, you should have three compost containers: one to be used for recent waste, one for waste that is in the process of rotting down, and one that contains compost that is ready for use. A three-section wooden bin is ideal (see diagram below).

A SECTIONED COMPOST BIN

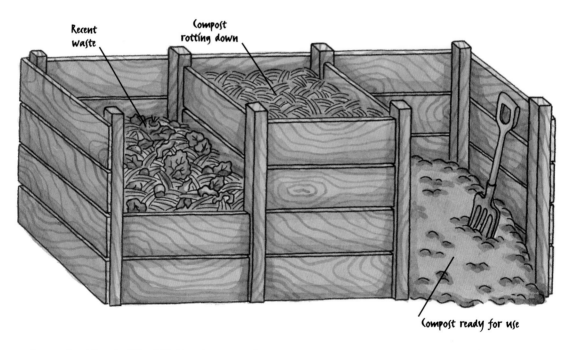

ABOVE **A compost container should be divided into three sections for compost in various stages of decay**

INSIDE A COMPOST BIN

Soft, sappy material, such as grass clippings, rot down first. These feed micro-organisms and speed up the composting. This activity increases heat. With the right balance, the compost can heat up to 140–158°F (60–70°C), hot enough to kill most weed seeds and some diseases. Once the soft material has been used up, the micro-organisms start to work on the woody material and the activity is decreased. The bin cools down and, if it is open at the bottom, other larger organisms, like worms and beetles, start to work. After a few months the contents of the bin become dark and crumbly and, once the woody material is broken down, it can be used in the garden. Shred woody material to increase the surface area available for micro-organisms to work on; this is important for a hot compost heap and quick compost.

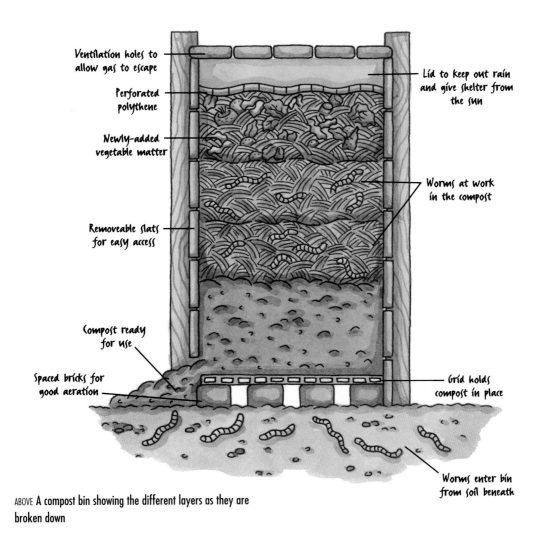

Ventilation holes to allow gas to escape

Perforated polythene

Newly-added vegetable matter

Removeable slats for easy access

Compost ready for use

Spaced bricks for good aeration

Lid to keep out rain and give shelter from the sun

Worms at work in the compost

Grid holds compost in place

Worms enter bin from soil beneath

ABOVE A compost bin showing the different layers as they are broken down

MATERIALS SUITABLE FOR COMPOSTING

Vegetable waste
Grass clippings
Kitchen waste (not meat, fish or cooked
 food as they will attract vermin)
Prunings (shred any woody ones first)
Pet manure and bedding (from vegetarian
 pets such as rabbits and guinea
 pigs only)
Dead flowers
Fruit skins
Nettles
Used tea bags
Torn paper and cardboard
Shredded brassica stems

ABOVE **Household waste for composting**

ABOVE **A trug filled with composting material**

MATERIALS UNSUITABLE FOR COMPOSTING

Clippings from lawns recently treated
 with weed killers
Chemically treated weeds
Hard objects – stones, bits of metal,
 plastic glass
Vacuum cleaner dust
Household/garden chemicals

COMPOSTING WITH A WORMERY

A wormery is a self-contained unit in which organic waste is broken down into a rich, dark compost by special compost worms. Wormeries are a good alternative to a compost heap if you live in a townhouse or apartment and have only kitchen waste to compost. They are small and can be kept in a garage or shed, or even indoors. You can buy both a wormery and the compost worms that activate it from garden suppliers. The worms will chomp their way through material many times their own weight and process it into rich castings, a process that is known as vermiculture. Worms thrive on a diet of former plant material, fruit and vegetable peelings, and they will also eat cereal, coffee grounds, stale bread and tea bags. The compost worms tackle a wide variety of waste and reduce its volume by up to 80 per cent, so they are also extremely practical. The worms create a useful compost for plants, and the liquid produced as part of the process can be drained off and used as a plant food. Wormeries are not expensive and there are a number of types to choose from.

ABOVE **Leaves for composting**

PLANTING FRUIT TREES

If a number of trees are to be planted, mark out the planting distances using canes. Dig a hole for each tree, making sure that is at least a third wider than its root system. Break up the subsoil to improve the drainage, and incorporate plenty of organic matter. Add one or two handfuls of organic blood, fish and bone meal fertilizer. Place a stake of an appropriate height in the hole, 3in (7.5cm) away from the centre. Tree varieties on dwarfing rootstocks will require permanent staking, but for other rootstocks the stakes can be removed after three years, once the tree is well established.

RIGHT **An apple tree ready for planting**

ABOVE **Digging a hole to plant a bare-rooted apple tree**

ABOVE **Driving in the stake to support the newly-planted tree**

Place the tree in the hole at the level of the soil mark on the stem, and spread out the roots. Backfill in stages, making sure the tree is upright. Firm the soil and level the area, and attach the tree to the stake using tree ties or strips of plastic. Water well and mulch with compost or manure. Surround with wire netting to protect it from animals. Container-grown trees can be planted at any time of year, if the weather is suitable.

Make sure you water your tree well during the first three years before it is established. Never plant stock when the conditions are freezing or waterlogged, or in uncultivated soil. Do not use wire or nylon twine ties as it will cut into the trunk and damage the tree as it grows.

RIGHT **Planting a bare-rooted apple tree**

ABOVE **Returning the soil after planting**

ABOVE **Putting a buckle tree tie in place**

ABOVE **Finished planting of 'Greensleeves' apple**

ABOVE **Apple tree 'Greensleeves' in flower**

PLANTING SOFT FRUITS

Fruit bushes have a more extensive root system. In late autumn to early spring, dig a hole deeper and wider than the spread roots. Loosen the bottom of the hole and set the plant in it. Fill with soil, giving the bush a gentle shake occasionally so the soil goes down and makes contact with the roots. Firm around the plant with your feet and rake over the soil until it is level.

Use a trowel to plant strawberry plants, digging a hole and placing the plants in it. The same principle applies to raspberry canes and blackberry plants, depending on how much root they have. If necessary use a small spade to plant them.

GARDEN PESTS AND DISEASES

Good husbandry is 90 per cent of successful organic gardening, and organic gardeners choose plants that are generally problem-free and grow them well. The organic approach is that of good cultivation practices – feeding the soil rather than the plants. Organic gardeners aim to keep their soil healthy, which in turn leads to healthy plants that are able to fend off minor pests and diseases that will inevitably occur. They strive to achieve a balance in their gardens so that chemicals are not required for pest and disease control. This results in much stronger plant growth, which is more able to cope with an attack if it does occur.

A plant that makes soft growth can be plagued by aphids which suck the sap from the leaves and shoots causing leaf curling and distortion, stunted growth and a black, sooty mould. These insects spread virus diseases from one plant to another, and can cause a considerable amount of damage.

Plants are much more susceptible to disease and pest infestation if they are overcrowded, weak and straggly, and under stress, so the best defence against such attack is to grow them in a well-prepared soil with added organic matter and the correct amount of nutrients and water. They also need spacious conditions where air and light can circulate – air circulation can be improved by planting at greater distances.

Restrict crop spraying to derris, pyrethrum and insecticidal soap, none of which have long-term damaging effects. Slugs tend to hide during the day, but a nocturnal hunt armed with a torch and a bucket of soapy water is one way of dealing with them. Or leave the skin of half a grapefruit or melon on the ground: slugs and snails hide under it and can be removed the following morning. You could try sinking a small dish half-filled with milk or beer into the ground. Slugs love these and will fall in and drown. Keep the container about 1in (2.5cm) above ground level or beneficial ground beetles may also be drowned. Creating a shady canopy of herbs will prove advantageous for foraging ground beetles that have an enormous appetite for slugs. Caterpillars, snails and green, black and mealy aphids can be picked off by hand.

Rubbish heaps, decaying crops and weeds can serve as hosts for many pests and diseases, as can dirty pots and seed trays, and soil brought into the greenhouse. Remove rotting leaves and debris from the floor and stick to a rigid hygiene regime.

LEFT **Diseased apple leaf**

COMPANION PLANTS IN THE GARDEN

Some plants seem healthier and more vigorous if they are grown alongside certain plants. These plants, which work in different ways, are known as companion plants and can be very useful in the fruit area. Organic gardeners use brightly-coloured, nectar and pollen rich flowers to encourage beneficial insects. One plant can help another by attracting or repelling insects

ABOVE Nettle is a good companion plant for soft fruit because it seems to improve its general health

that will pollinate or damage it. Many plants release a repellent gas or aroma from their foliage, flowers or roots. Others may condition or feed the soil, or directly affect it by releasing nitrogen, for example, and making it available to other plants. A plant might help to create the right microclimate for its neighbour. The cottage garden tradition of interplanting vegetables, herbs and flowers is extremely practical. The different scents confuse pests and cause less damage to the soil than monocropping. Planting herbs, plus nectar- and pollen-rich flowers in your fruit garden will deter pests and attract insects that are valuable pollinators, or that prey on common garden pests. Planting marigolds, nasturtiums, poppies and convolvulus between other plants will control aphids by attracting beneficial insects like hoverflies that prey on them. They will lay their eggs in aphid colonies and their larvae will feed on them. Tobacco plants will trap small insects on their sticky stems.

ABOVE Poppies help to control aphids by attracting insects that eat them

ENCOURAGING WILDLIFE

Organic gardens can be paradises for wildlife. Grow a range of plants and flowers that will provide food and shelter to attract as wide a range as possible. Attracting natural predators into your garden will work for you by helping to keep pests under control. A small patch of flowering wildflowers will attract butterflies and bees. Birds can be encouraged using a bird bath and nesting boxes, and they will eat grubs, slugs, aphids and caterpillars. A garden pond will encourage frogs and toads that will feed off small insects, woodlice and slugs. Grow a wide variety of plants to attract ladybirds and their larvae which feed off aphids, as do lacewing larvae.

ABOVE **Hoverflies are attracted to marigolds**

ABOVE **Sunflowers will attract parasitic wasps**

ABOVE **Borage is a magnet for bees**

GROUND COVER

Provide ground cover plants and organic mulch to attract ground beetles and centipedes. Dead nettles act as valuable cover for predators such as frogs and beetles. Centipedes feed on small insects and slugs and ground beetles come out during the night to eat eelworms, cutworms, leather jackets and insect eggs and larvae. Hedgehogs will emerge from ground cover at dusk, and will happily devour millipedes, cutworms, slugs, wireworms and woodlice.

OPPOSITE BELOW **The buddleia has beautiful flowers and is also known as the butterfly bush**

ABOVE **Chamomile will attract snails**

SECTION TWO

LEFT **Fruit trees adjoining the vegetable patch**

CHAPTER 5

A–Z plant directory

This directory does not claim to be an exhaustive list of fruit, but my selection will allow you to grow a good variety, wherever you live. Individual types of fruit are listed alphabetically with all the information you will need to get started. Popular varieties are listed after each fruit, with suitable companion plants where appropriate. Nuts are a class of fruit that usually consists of a single edible kernel enclosed in a hard shell, for example almonds, pecans and cobnuts. Botanically, nuts are simple dry fruits, and most are the seeds of trees. Commercially, the term nuts is applied to many fruits with hard outer shells or coverings, including leguminous pods such as peanuts.

NAMING OF PLANTS

If the description of the fruit is in italics, this is a naturally-occurring plant discovered growing in habitat. In *Ribes nigrum,* for example, *Ribes* is the genus name and *nigrum* is the species name. The plant was originally found growing in Europe and Asia, and is therefore a true species. Botanists may find slight variations, so if you see the terms f. or var. or subsp. they describe naturally-occurring forms, varieties and subspecies. If, however, you see a description like Ribes nigrum 'Ben Gairn', it means the plant is a cultivar; plant breeders and hybridizers have been selecting and crossing plants to produce a distinctive plant that they can name. If a plant description has 'xxxx' after any name, it is a cultivar rather than a true species.

HARDINESS RATINGS

The information given is based on UK Royal Horticultural Society data, but is on the cautious side. If you are not prepared to take any chances, follow the hardiness rating to the letter. Otherwise, there is a great deal of leeway. Raised beds, good drainage, south-/south-west facing borders and planting against a house wall all give plants a better habitat – so be prepared to experiment. If you cannot bear the thought of losing your most valued plants, keep back-ups by taking cuttings or dividing the plants and growing spares, perhaps in a different part of the garden.

Half-hardy: down to 32° F/0° C
Frost-hardy: down to 23° F/−5° C
Fully hardy: down to 5° F/−15° C
(FT) Frost tender

SAFETY WARNING:

Many plants can be harmful, both if eaten and as skin irritants, or because they are allergens and may aggravate asthma, eczema and other auto-immune disorders. Do not eat them unless you are certain that they have a culinary use. Be wary of skin contact, especially in bright sunlight. Tell children never to eat anything from the garden unless you have given it to them!

NAME: ALMOND
PRUNUS DULCIS
FAMILY: ROSACEAE

Type: Perennial

USDA zone: 7–9

Description: The almond is similar in form to the peach, but blossoms earlier. Usually pruned and trained as a bush, it produces light pink blossom and fruits with tough, leathery, greenish-brown skin. The kernel of the nut is flat, oval and pointed. Almonds are grown widely in California, South Australia and South Africa. They are only partially self-fertile.

Where to grow: Almonds prefer a light, rich, well-drained soil (pH 6.5) and a sheltered frost-free position. They can be grown in containers and kept under glass in winter and through their flowering period.

When to plant: During the dormant season from late autumn until early spring.

How to grow: Prepare the ground well before planting and dress with organic fertilizer. Dig a hole wide and deep enough to take the roots of the tree when extended. After planting apply a 2–3in (57.5cm) deep mulch around the tree. Plant the trees 20–22ft (6–7m) apart and stake during the first year. Cross pollinating varieties may have to be planted to produce a crop.

Maintenance: Water until established and mulch with well-rotted manure. Protect blossom from frost and spray regularly with seaweed solution. Thin the fruits in early summer.

Pruning and training: In early spring of the first year, shorten three or four laterals by two-thirds, cutting back to an outward facing bud. Trim back any unwanted laterals. In summer, prune back the leader to the topmost lateral, and any side shoots below the main laterals. Remove any shoots growing inward or down. In early spring of the second year cut weak sub-laterals to 4in (10cm). To form the main branches, halve the length of the strongest laterals and sub-laterals, before bud-break.

Established bushes: In early summer, cut back about a quarter of the shoots that have fruited to a replacement bud or shoot. Remove any crossed branches and old, decayed, diseased and unproductive wood.

Propagation: Almonds can be propagated from stones but will take years to fruit, so are usually increased by chip-budding. Rootstocks vary depending on soil type, but seedling almond or peach rootstocks are often used.

Harvesting and storing: The trees bear fruit after three of four years. Harvest the almonds when their shells start to crack. They can be stored in dry salt for long periods.

Average yield: 20lb (9kg) of almonds from an established tree.

Pests and diseases: Earwigs, squirrels and rabbits. Peach leaf curl.

Recommended varieties:

'Macrocarpa' is the best fruiting variety.

'Ayles' is a self-fertile variety.

'Ferraduel' is a partially self-fertile variety.

Companion plants: Garlic, chives, clover, nettles planted close by.

ABOVE **Almond tree in bloom**

NAME: **APPLE**
MALUS SYLVESTRIS VAR. DOMESTICA
FAMILY: **ROSACEAE**

Type: Hardy perennial

USDA zone: 6–8

Description: Innumerable varieties of apple are grown all over the world. They flower in late spring and fruit in late summer and autumn, and a tree can fruit for 30 years. The two types are tip-bearers (fruit develops near the tip of the shoots), and spur-bearers (fruit found on older wood).

Where to grow: Apples will grow in almost any deep, well-drained, slightly acid (pH 6.7) soil, but dwarfing rootstocks like a more fertile soil. All apples prefer a sunny, frost-free site sheltered from winds, though they will tolerate some shade. M27 and M9 rootstocks can be grown in containers.

When to plant: Plant when dormant, preferably in autumn while the soil is still warm.

How to grow: Choose early-ripening cultivars for shaded gardens and cool temperatures, and late-flowering ones where there are late frosts. Plant to the same depth as at the nursery. Spread the roots well. Planting distances depend on the vigour of the selected cultivars and rootstocks, and how they will be trained. Use stakes and tree ties for half-standards, standards, bush trees and spindlebushes (central-leaders). Fit supports and wires before planting, and fit stakes on all untrained trees.

Maintenance: In dry weather, water any newly-planted trees thoroughly. Water trees in fruit well, or yield will be smaller and there will be fewer fruit buds the next year. In early spring, apply organic fertiizer to the soil under the branches. In mid-spring, mulch round the base of the trunk with rotted manure or compost, keeping it away from the bark. Thin if heavy crops have set, and after the normal early summer drop if the crop is still heavy.

Pruning and training: Cut out dead and diseased wood to maintain shape and openness. Prune larger trees in winter, and those with a more controlled shape in both summer and winter.

Bush and standard (two-year-old) trees: In late autumn to early spring of the second year, keep four primary branches. Cut back to half their length strong branches, and less-vigorous ones to a third of their length. Cut to outward-facing buds. In late autumn to early spring of the third year, keep four more new growths for permanent branches. Cut back vigorous growth to a third of its length, to outward-facing buds. Prune new growth to keep the tree open at the centre.

Established trees: Cease leader pruning in late autumn to early spring. Leave laterals on the outer part of the tree unpruned. Cut back inside laterals to about 4in (10cm).

Tip-bearers: Remove all crossing, dead and diseased wood. Leave laterals with fruit buds at their tips, but cut back some of the leaders.

Spur-bearers: Remove all crossing, dead and diseased wood. Cut back any overcrowded laterals in the centre. Do not prune leaders inside the head, but prune all laterals growing into the branch leader. Do not prune leaders and laterals outside the head. Thin fruiting spurs if necessary. If you have undersized fruit or overcropping, cut out some of the laterals.

Espalier (maiden whip): During the first winter, cut back the stem to 15in (37.5cm) above a bud that has two good buds below. In summer, train the shoot from the top bud vertically up the cane and tie as it develops. Tie two main laterals to canes attached at an angle of 45° to the wires. Cut back any laterals that have grown below these two main arms to 2–3 leaves. During the winter of the second year, lower the two side branches to horizontal and tie them to the wire. To form the second tier, cut the main stem to just above the second wire, leaving two strong buds below it. Cut back the two horizontals of the first tier to two-thirds of their length, to a downward-facing bud. In the summer of the second year, tie the developing shoots of the second tier and the extension shoots of the first tier to canes. Prune the laterals on the stem between the first and second tiers to three buds. Cut back any sub-laterals more than 9in (23cm) long on the tiers to 3 or 4 leaves.

Established espalier: In summer, prune back the new terminal growths of the vertical and horizontal arms to the start of their new growth.

Cordon: In winter/spring, plant a maiden tree against a cane tied at 45° to a wire system . Tie the main stem to it. Cut back the side shoots to four buds. Do not prune the leader. In the second and subsequent years, remove flowers in spring from the spurs that have formed on the pruned side shoots. In summer, prune to three leaves any laterals longer than 9in (23cm) that arise from the stem. Cut back the lateral side shoots from existing spur systems to one leaf beyond the basal cluster.

Propagation: Usually by grafting.

Harvesting and storing: Pick fruit daily when ripe. Never tug from the tree as this may damage the spurs. Early varieties cannot be stored and mid-season ones will keep for a few weeks. Late varieties store well, in an airy place, in stacked trays with a ventilation space between each. Wrap each fruit in oiled paper and place folded side down on the tray.

Average yields: Bush 30–50lb (15–25kg); espalier/fan 20–25lb (10–11.3kg); cordon 6–12lb (2.7–5.4kg).

Pests and diseases: Birds, greenfly, woolly aphids, codling moths, wasps. Canker, scab, powdery mildew, brown rot, bitter pit.

Recommended varieties:

Eating apples: 'Saturn' (organic) is a disease-resistant variety that crops in mid-autumn. The conical apples are flushed red over a green-yellow background.

'Fiesta' (organic) has flushed, bright red skin that crops in mid-autumn. It is a good cropper and suitable for colder areas.

'Greensleeves' is a hardy, reliable, self-fertile variety with pale green fruits that turn yellow.

'Worcester Pearmain' (organic) is a reliable early autumn cropper with a sweet flavour and flushed, bright red skin. It is a good pollinator and a partial tip bearer.

Cooking apples: 'Bramley's Seedling' (organic) is a good cooker that crops in mid autumn. It is not a good pollinator.

'Howgate Wonder' (organic) is a mid-autumn cropper with very large, pale green fruits that become yellow and partly flushed and striped with brownish red.

'Arthur Turner' (organic) is a large, hardy, mid-autumn cropper. It is prone to mildew but fairly resistant to scab, and is partially self-fertile.

Companion plants: Chives, horseradish, garlic, tansy.

ABOVE 'Granny Smith' apples

NAME: **APRICOT**
PRUNUS ARMENIACA
FAMILY: **ROSACEAE**

Type: Hardy perennial

USDA zone: 9–10

Description: Apricots have downy orange, pale orange or golden-yellow skins, often flushed with red. They are grown on the plum rootstock 'St Julien A' or on seedling peach or seedling apricot rootstocks. Apricots are self-fertile, but the flowers should be pollinated by hand. They are grown widely in California and Australia.

Where to grow: Apricots prefer a moisture-retentive but well-drained, slightly alkaline soil (pH 6.5–8). They also enjoy a sunny, sheltered, frost-free site. In cooler areas grow them against a sunny wall or in a greenhouse.

ABOVE **The golden-yellow, downy-skinned fruits of the apricot tree**

When to plant: Plant in late autumn or very early winter in well prepared ground.

How to grow: Prepare the ground in autumn, incorporating plenty of well-rotted manure or compost. Plant bare-rooted plants in late autumn, staking bush trees for the first two years. Plant fan-trained trees 6in (15cm) from the wall or fence and 15ft (4.5m) apart. Plant bush trees 10–15ft (3–4.5m) apart.

Maintenance: Water regularly if the weather is dry. The fruit will need thinning at intervals, starting when the apricots are the size of a cherry until the fruits are almost full size. Thin until they are 2–3in (5–7.5cm) apart. If necessary protect the blossom from frost damage by covering with netting at night. Apply a general organic fertilizer in late winter.

Pruning and training: For bushes, follow the procedure for plums (see page 145). For fans, follow the procedure for peach fans (see page 137). For established fan-trained trees follow the procedure for plum fans (see page 145).

Propagation: By chip-budding or T-budding, using 'St Julien A' or seedling peach rootstocks.

Harvesting and storing: Pick when fully ripe. Fruit will come away from its stalk easily but it bruises easily so handle carefully. They can be kept for several weeks in a cool place, or dried, bottled or frozen (remove stones).

Average yields: Bush 30–100lb (13.5–45.5kg) Fan 12–35lb (5.4–16kg).

Pests and diseases: Aphids, red spider mite, silver leaf, bacterial canker, apricot die-back.

Recommended varieties:

'Moorpark' is a popular variety with large fruits that ripen in late summer.

'Farmingdale' is a good cropper with juicy, orange flesh. Fruits ripen in mid/late summer.

'Hemskerke' is an early variety that succeeds well in cooler areas.

Companion plants: Garlic, chives, basil, marigold, nasturtium.

NAME: **AVOCADO PEAR**
PERSEA AMERICANA
FAMILY: **LAURACEAE**

Type: Subtropical evergreen

USDA zone: 10–11

Description: Avocados have green-black, knobbly fruit and fairly dense foliage. They can reach 80ft (24m). The main types are West Indian, Guatemalan and Mexican. Flowers, which attract hoverflies, appear in clusters of up to 300 in winter, but only 2–3 fruits will develop. Flower types are type A, which is receptive to pollen in the morning and releases it the following afternoon, and type B which releases pollen in the morning and is receptive to it the next afternoon. Fruit sets best when plants are cross-pollinated between A and B.

Where to grow: Avocados prefer light, loose soil and full sun, and grow well on hillsides. They will tolerate shade but fruit production will suffer. For the blooms to set, cool temperatures of 40–55°F (5–13°C) are needed.

When to plant: Set out the plants in spring, digging holes large enough to take the roots when extended. Plant out container-grown plants any time, if the weather is suitable.

How to grow: Avocados may be self-fertile, but for the best crop production plant two cultivars near each other. Allow 20ft (6m) each way between trees.

Growing under glass: Plant in well-prepared greenhouse border beds or 10in (25cm) pots. Young plants need a temperature of 68–82°F (20–28°C) and 70 per cent humidity.

Maintenance: Water container-grown plants regularly and feed with an organic liquid feed every 1–2 weeks. In temperate climates, plants are unlikely to flower or fruit under glass because they need high light intensity. The roots grow fast and if allowed will take over nearby plants. Ease off watering in winter as overwatering can cause root rot. Protect outdoor plants from frost.

Pruning: Prune into shape during early growth. Remove any damaged, diseased or crossing branches after fruiting in established plants.

Propagation: Usually by grafting, but may be grown from seed. Remove the seed from the avocado and soak in hot water for 30–45 minutes to combat infection. Cut a thin slice from the pointed end and dip it in fungicide. Sow seed in a pot of sandy compost with the cut end slightly above the surface. Germination usually takes around a month. Transplant young plants into their final positions when they are about 12–16in (30–40cm) high.

Harvesting and storing: Cut slightly underripe fruit with secateurs. Ripen at about 45°F (7°C) with 60 per cent humidity. Grafted varieties produce fruit at 3–5 years old, seed-raised varieties at 5–7 years old. Fruits can remain on the tree for more than a year without maturing.

ABOVE **Avocado pear plant**

ABOVE **Avocado pear**

Average yields: 120 fruits per tree per year.
Pests and diseases: Red spider mite, whitefly, thrips, mealy bugs, fungal leaf spots, avocado root rot.
Recommended varieties:
'Fuerte' (*Mexico*) has large, dark green fruit with small raised spots and tends to fruit only in alternate years.
'Hass' (*Guatemala*) is a rather open tree with medium-sized fruits that have thick, pebbled, coppery purple skin.
'Nabal' (*Antigua, Guatemala*) is a columnar tree with green-skinned fruit and excellent flesh.
'Lula' (*Guatemala*) is a dense, prolific tree with round, green, glossy fruits that have slightly rough skin.
Companion plants: None known.

NAME: **BANANA**
MUSA SPP
FAMILY: **MUSACEAE**

Type: Perennial
USDA zone: 8–11
Description: Banana plants have large, oblong leaves up to 15ft (4.5m) long. The 'stem' is a tightly-wound sheath of leaves. It dies down to the ground after fruiting and is replaced by others growing up from the rhizome. Flowers appear in groups or hands along the stem. The first to appear contain female flowers that will develop into bananas which are green at first and ripen to yellow or red. The flesh is creamy-yellow with a rich, sweet flavour.
Where to grow: Bananas require a deep, rich, heavy, well-drained soil with lots of moisture (pH 5.5–7) and a sunny, sheltered site. In cooler climates the Chinese banana (*Musa cavendishii*) is suited to growing under glass and in containers. *Musa basjoo* can withstand temperatures of 23–17°F (–5 to –8°C).
When to plant: At any time of the year.

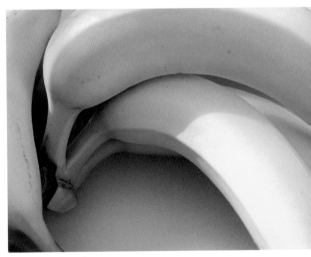

ABOVE **Bunch of ripe bananas**

How to grow: Banana plants are easily raised from seed, which are the size of large marbles. Space the smallest varieties 8–10ft (2.4–3m) apart. The banana tree makes a striking specimen plant, and for ornamental purposes can be planted as close as 2–3ft (60–90cm) apart. They do not need cross-pollination.

Maintenance: Water regularly in hot weather. Fertilize at regular intervals during the growing season. They are dormant in winter. Cut off the male flowers from the far end of the fruit stalk. Keep plants grown under glass at a temperature above 65°F (18°C) in winter and under 85°F (29°C) in summer. Container-grown plants can be put outside in summer. Cover outside plants with straw in winter. Wrap wire mesh around the bottom of the plant leaving a gap of about 10in (25cm) between it and the stem. Fill the mesh to the top with straw and twist the ends together. Repeat for the top part of the plant, but leave a 15in (37.5cm) gap between it and the stem. Tie the two lots of mesh together with string and fill the top piece with straw.

Pruning and training: A banana stem will flower and fruit in around 18 months and continue fruiting if well-tended. Remove all but one main shoot and a replacement. Cut out the main shoot when it has fruited.

Propagation: Ornamental varieties from seed; edible varieties from pieces of rhizome with a bud, or by suckers.

Harvesting and storing: When the fruits begin to change colour, cut off the whole stalk and ripen at room temperature. Bananas are best eaten fresh, but can be dried.

Average yields: 6–8 hands per stem from well-tended plants.

Pests and diseases: Few problems.

ABOVE **Banana tree in container**

Recommended varieties:
'Robusta' is a tall variety that needs hot, moist conditions to grow well.
'William' is a medium, more productive hybrid.
'Lady Finger' is a standard size plant that bears thin-skinned fruit.
'Apple' is similar to 'Lady Finger' except that its fruits have a 'fresh apple' aftertaste.
Companion plants: None known.

NAME: **BLACKBERRY**
RUBUS FRUTICOSUS
FAMILY: **ROSACEAE**

Type: Perennial

USDA zone: 6–8

Description: Blackberries fruit over a long season. Fruits are borne on canes in late summer. The thornless cultivars are not as vigorous. Blackberries are self-fertile.

Where to grow: Choose an area that has not grown raspberries or blackberries for a number of years. Blackberries grow best in well-drained soil (pH about 6.5). They produce the best fruits in full sun, but will tolerate some shade. Provide some shelter in cold or exposed areas, as they are prone to damage from hard winter frosts. Plant against a sunny sheltered wall or fence, using a strong support system. Canes that fruited during the previous summer/autumn must be supported in addition to this season's canes for fruiting next year.

When to plant: Bare-rooted canes are best planted in late autumn/early winter or in early spring. Plant container-grown plants at any time of the year, when weather permits.

How to grow: Prepare the ground thoroughly before planting, incorporating plenty of organic matter. Place the canes 12–15ft (3.5–4.5m) apart (thornless varieties can be closer), then shorten them to a bud about 9–12in (23–30cm) above the ground. Blackberries do not like deep planting so just cover the roots.

Maintenance: Water in dry weather. Mulch in the spring. Blackberries need high nitrogen so feed with an organic fertilizer in early spring.

Pruning and training: By the end of the first season, the number of branches will have at least doubled. Cut some of them back – the number will depend on how many have been produced – to just above the base. Trim off any weak shoots. Every following year cut back about a third of all shoots to just above the base. Also cut off any damaged or weak wood, and tie in the new growth.

Propagation: Bend down a vigorous shoot and plant its tip to form a layer. When a new plant has formed, sever it from the parent plant.

Harvesting and storing: Pick the fruit as it ripens from late summer until the first frosts. It is better to use the fruit straight away, but it can be frozen, bottled or used in preserves.

Average yield: 12–15lb (5.4–6.8kg) per bush.

Possible pests and diseases: Raspberry beetles, birds, grey mould (*botrytis*).

Recommended varieties:

'Bedford Giant' is an early variety with very long canes and a good flavour.

'Oregon Thornless' is a thornless variety with quite a good flavour, that is easy to train.

'John Innes' is a later variety with extra-large jet-black shiny fruits. It is not quite so vigorous.

Companion plants: Tansy, stinging nettles.

ABOVE **Wild blackberries**

NAME: **BLACKCURRANT**
RIBES NIGRUM
FAMILY: **GROSSULARIACEAE**

Type: Perennial

USDA zone: 6–8

Description: Blackcurrants have dark purple, almost black, berries with an aromatic smell and aromatic leaves and stems. They are self-fertile, and grow on a stool system (many shoots spring from below ground rather than from a single stem).

Where to grow: Blackcurrants prefer a deep, organic-rich, moisture retentive soil (pH 6.5–7). Avoid soil that is wet or poorly drained. Lime very acid soil.

When to plant: Plant bare-rooted bushes in late autumn or in late winter/early spring. Container grown plants can be planted when the weather is suitable at any time of the year.

How to grow: Plant the canes 5ft (1.5m) apart in rows 5ft (1.5m) apart.

Maintenance: Mulch in spring with well-rotted manure and apply an organic fertilizer. Water in dry weather. Stop watering as the fruits begin to ripen or the skins may split. Net bushes to protect them from bird damage.

Pruning and training: Planted deeply, blackcurrants send up new shoots from below soil level every year. To avoid congestion, prune the oldest (dark) stems to soil level in winter. Stems darken in colour after three or four years and must be removed to make room for young, productive shoots that will produce flowers in spring and crop in mid summer.

Propagation: Take hardwood cuttings 8–10in (20–25cm) long from healthy bushes in autumn. Keep all the buds intact to encourage basal shoots. Insert the cuttings into a trench leaving two buds exposed above ground level.

Harvesting and storing: Harvest ripe, dry, firm fruits in bunches. It can be eaten fresh, bottled, made into jam, or frozen.

ABOVE **Blackcurrants**

Average yields: 10lb (4.5kg) per bush.

Pests and diseases: Aphids, gall mites, big bud mites, winter moth caterpillars, birds, grey mould (*botrytis*), powdery mildew, fungal leaf spot.

Recommended varieties:

Early: 'Ben Gairn' (organic) has excellent disease resistance and is good for organic growing.

'Ben Connan' (organic) is a high-yielding variety with very large berries.

Late: 'Ben Alder' (organic) A variety widely grown for juice production. Its compact and upright bushes grow to 4ft (1.2m) high.

Companion plants: Nettles.

NAME: **BLUEBERRY**
VACCINIUM CORYMBOSUM
FAMILY: **ERICACEAE**

Type: Perennial

USDA zone: 6–8

Description: Highbush blueberries (known as blueberries) are descendants of the American wild blueberry and members of the heather family. They require a cool, moist climate. The bushes bear white flowers in spring followed by clusters of dark, purple-black fruits with a grey bloom, and gold and scarlet autumn colour. They are partially self-fertile but do better when grown with other varieties.

Where to grow: Blueberries prefer moist, free-draining soil (pH 4.5 or less). Add liberal amounts of moss peat or acid leaf-mould to acid, sandy or clay soils. They like sun, but will tolerate some shade. They can also be grown in 12–15in (30–37.5cm) pots filled with ericaceous compost.

When to plant: Plant container-grown bushes in spring or autumn.

How to grow: Dig holes 12in (30cm) deep and wide. Fill with equal parts of leaf mould and soil, or peat and soil. Blueberries thrive when associated with a fungus that flourishes where organic matter is plentiful. Organic fertilizer may be added. Plant the bushes 5ft (1.5m) apart in rows 6ft (1.8m) apart. Make a hole with a trowel in the prepared planting position, big enough to take the root ball. Set the plant in it and firm the soil.

Maintenance: Apply a dressing of hoof and horn in spring. Mulch with an acid compost and water with rain water, not tap water. Weed carefully, and net to protect from birds.

Pruning and training: Little needed for 2–3 years. Subsequently, cut back damaged or dead branches close to the wood during the dormant period. Cut back some of the branches that have become twiggy.

ABOVE **Blueberry bushes bear white flowers in spring**

INSET **Ripe blueberries**

ABOVE **A blueberry growing in a container**

Propagation: Take softwood cuttings 4–6in (10–15cm) long in mid-summer and insert in an acidic rooting medium. Root in a propagator, then transplant into larger pots. Harden cuttings off before planting out.

Harvesting and storing: Pick the berries, which ripen over a period of several weeks, when ripe and starting to soften. Eat fresh, bottle, freeze, or make into jam.

Average yields: 6lb (2.7kg) per bush.

Pests and diseases: Few, though in the US various grubs attack the fruit.

Recommended varieties:

Early: 'Earliblue' is fairly compact variety. 'Blue Crop' is a more upright variety.

Mid-season: 'Berkeley' is a spreading variety.

Late: 'Jersey' is a fairly compact variety.

Companion plants: Heathers.

NAME: CAPE GOOSEBERRY – DWARF PHYSALIS PRUINOSA
FAMILY: SOLANACEAE

Type: Perennial

USDA zone: All zones

Description: The cape gooseberry is an herbaceous perennial with a bushy habit and branching stems. It is cultivated like a tomato. The exotic bright yellow/orange fruit, borne in late summer/autumn, is covered with papery husks that protects it from pests. There is also a larger growing variety *Physalis peruviana*.

Where to grow: Cape gooseberry can be grown as an annual wherever you can grow tomatoes. It needs a sunny position and well-drained, rich, light soil. It grows well in containers and growing bags and can also be planted in the ornamental border.

When to plant: Sow seed under glass in spring after the last frosts.

How to grow: Sow seed in a tray on the surface of a good, free-draining compost and cover with a sieved sprinkling of the same compost. If possible, place the tray in a propagator at a temperature of 64–70°F (18–21°C). It will take 2–3 weeks to germinate. When the seedlings are large enough to handle, transplant into 3in (7.5cm) pots and continue to grow at a temperature of 59°F (15°C). When the young plants are 8in (20cm) high, harden them off and plant them out at a distance of 3ft (90cm) apart. They can also be planted singly in 12in (30cm) pots, or two plants to a growing bag.

Maintenance: Support plants if necessary. Pinch out new shoots to encourage bushy growth. In spring, mulch with well-rotted organic matter and feed with a balanced organic fertilizer.

Pruning and training: No drastic pruning is necessary. Tie in loose growth and cut back withered stems after cropping. Cut the plants back hard after the first harvest.

ABOVE **Ripe Cape Gooseberry**

Propagation: From seed. Perennial varieties can be increased by root cuttings or division during spring. Yields of perennials will be better if the plants are replaced every 2–3 years.

Harvesting and storing: Let the fruit ripen until a full yellow-orange colour can be seen through the husks, which should be dry and papery. It can be stored for months if kept dry and in its husks. The husks must be removed before eating.

Average yields: 300 fruits per plant.

Pests and diseases: No significant problems.

Recommended varieties:

'Golden Berry' has tangy, delicious fruit that is ready to harvest when the calyx turns brown.

'Little Lantern' is compact with a spreading habit.

Physalis peruviana:

'Golden Berry' bears rich, golden fruit.

'Giant Poha Berry' is 12–30in (30–45cm) tall with fuzzy, grey-green leaves.

Companion plants: None known.

NAME: CHERRY (SWEET)
PRUNUS AVIUM
FAMILY: ROSACEAE

Type: Perennial

USDA zone: 6–8

Description: Sweet cherry trees bear clusters of white flowers in spring and can reach 25ft (7.5m). Fruit colour ranges from near black to pale yellow, with flesh that is either firm and moist or soft and juicy. The trees are not self-fertile so choose cultivars that pollinate each other. The 'Duke' cherry is thought to be a cross between the sweet and acid cherry.

Where to grow: Cherries need deep, well-drained soil (pH 6.5–7.5) and an open, sunny, sheltered position. Blossom is susceptible to frost and young trees can be damaged by wind. Plant fan-trained trees against a wall.

When to plant: Plant bare-rooted sweet cherries in late autumn or winter. Plant container-grown plants at any time if the weather is suitable.

How to grow: Prepare the soil before planting. For bare-rooted trees, dig a hole wide enough to take the roots when extended. Drive in a stake to reach just below the lowest branches, two stakes and a crossbar for standard cherries. Fan-trained trees will need a horizontal wire support with the wires spaced at 6in (15cm), at least 8ft (2.4m) high and 15ft (4.5m) wide. Plant the tree to the same planting depth as previously. Fill the hole with soil and firm. Tie standard varieties to the stake with a tree tie and tie in the branches of the fan to the wall wires.

Planting distances/row spacing:

Standard F12/1: 35ft (10.5m)/35ft (10.5m).

Half-standard F12/1: 25ft (7.5m)/25ft (7.5m).

Bush F12/1: 25ft (7.5m)/25ft (7.5m).

Fan F12/1: 20ft (6m) apart.

Bush colt: 15ft (4.5m) /15ft (4.5m).

Fan colt: 12ft (3.6m)/12ft (3.6m).

Maintenance: Water regularly in dry weather as fruits may split if watering is irregular. Keep grass away from the trunk, particularly during the first four years when it is best to keep it 2–3ft (30–90cm) away. Net to prevent bird damage, and drape netting over the bushes or fans in spring to help to protect them from frost.

Pruning and training: Sweet cherries fruit on spurs of the wood of trees aged two or more.

Fan-trained trees: Fix two canes to the wires at a 35° angle in the spring of the first year and tie two string laterals to them. In the spring of the second year, choose suitable buds and prune each leader to 12in (30cm). Use shoots that will develop in the summer for the fan ribs. In the spring of the third year, cut back all leaders to suitable buds so there is about 18in (45cm) of new growth. In spring of the fourth year onwards, by which time most of the wall space will have been filled, cut out any laterals growing towards the wall. In mid-summer, cut back to six leaves any laterals not required for the framework. When the tree reaches the top of the wall, bend and tie down the shoots. In mid-autumn, cut back to three leaves the laterals that were cut back in mid-summer. This will ensure the formation of fruit buds at the base of the shoots in the following year.

Bush and half-standards: Cut back three or four laterals to a third of their length in the spring of the first year. Cut to outward facing buds and remove any laterals below the selected ones. Cut the leader above the topmost lateral at an angle. In spring of the second year, cut back by half three or four of the strongest sub-laterals that have developed from the laterals forming the framework. Prune out any weak or badly-positioned laterals. On a mature bush, cut back any dead, damaged or unproductive laterals in summer to a suitable replacement shoot, to encourage the formation of fruit buds.

ABOVE **Cherry blossom in spring**
INSET **Ripe juicy cherries**

Propagation: By chip- or T-budding or by grafting on to rootstocks.

Harvesting and storing: Pick the cherries with their stalks on when ripe, using scissors or secateurs to remove them. They should be sweet and juicy and eaten as soon as possible after harvesting. If the cherries start to crack, pick them at once. Sweet cherries can be frozen, the red and black ones are the best.

Average yields: Fan 12–35lb (5.4–17.3kg) per tree; bush 30–100lb (13.6–45.5kg).

Pests and diseases: Caterpillars, cherry black fly, birds, bacterial canker, silver leaf, brown rot.

Recommended varieties:

'Bigarreau Gaucher' (organic) is an old variety that flowers from mid to late season. It has almost black fruits with very dark red, juicy flesh.
'Merton Glory' (organic) is a 'white' dessert cherry with fairly large, white fruit, flushed red. It is a vigorous and regular cropper.
'May Duke' (organic) is a mid-season cherry with dark red skin and soft juicy flesh. It is only partially self-fertile.
'Early Rivers' (organic) is an early cropper, with red-black, shiny skin and dark red, juicy flesh.

Companion plants: Clover, alfalfa, chives, marigolds, lettuce, nasturtium, spinach.

NAME: **COBNUTS AND FILBERTS**
CORYLUS AVELLANA / CORYLUS MAXIMA
FAMILY: **CORYLACEAE**

Type: Perennial
USDA zone: 6–9
Description: Both cobnuts and filberts are bushy trees with dark stems bearing separate clusters of male (catkins) and tiny red female flowers on the same tree. Both are wind-pollinated. Cobnut catkins are yellow and filbert catkins range from yellow-green to red. Both appear in early spring. Trees bear nuts after 3–4 years.
Where to grow: Cobnuts and filberts will grow on almost any soil, but need good drainage. Rich soil can cause vigorous leaf growth and poor crops – pH6 is about right. Both tolerate light shade and require a sheltered position.
When to plant: Autumn or early winter.
How to grow: Plant two- or three-year-old stock on prepared ground 15ft (4.5m) apart. Dig a hole wide and deep enough to take the roots when extended. Drive in a stake to reach just below the lowest branch. Plant to the depth of the original soil level, refill the hole, and firm. Tie the tree to the stake with a tree tie.

RIGHT **Ripening cobnuts**

ABOVE **Mature Kent cobnut trees growing in the 'Garden of England'**
INSET **Ripe, harvested cobnuts**

Maintenance: Keep weed free, water well in dry weather and mulch regularly. In spring, apply organic fertilizer to poor soils.

Pruning and training: Grow in bush form with a 15–18in (37.5–45cm) main stem and eight to ten main branches. In late winter, cut back leaders by about half to an outward facing bud, so good laterals will develop, and remove low-growing shoots. Prune all but the strongest shoots (needed to develop the framework), shortening to two-thirds of their length. Do not prune laterals bearing female flowers. In late summer, break the longer side shoots to about half their length and leave them hanging. This technique, known as brutting, lets air and light into the tree. Brutted side shoots are usually cut back a further 2–3in (5–7.5cm) in winter.

Propagation: By suckers from the roots, or layering.

Harvesting and storing: Harvest when the husks begin to turn yellow. Dry and store.

Average yields: About 25lb (11.3kg) per tree.

Pests and diseases: Squirrels.

Recommended varieties:

Cobnuts: 'Longue d'Espagne' (organic), an old variety with very long, large nuts, is often known as Kent Cob.

'Cosford Cob' (organic) produces excellent, thin-shelled fruit and prolific pollen.

Filberts: 'White Filbert' is a traditional variety.

'Red Filbert' (organic) has reddish-tinted leaves, husks and skins.

Companion plants: Primroses and bluebells.

NAME: **CRANBERRY**
VACCINIUM OXYCOCCUS
FAMILY: **ERICACEAE**

Type: Evergreen

USDA zone: 5–6

Description: Cranberries grow as low bushes with long, wiry stems and pointed, narrow leaves. They bear clusters of small, pink flowers and masses of red or pink berries, some with brown-red spots. They are self-fertile.

Where to grow: Cranberries do well in a moist, acid soil with a high organic content and a pH of 3–4.5. Moss peat can be forked into the top of the soil or a cranberry bed can be prepared. They need a sunny position.

When to plant: In autumn, mild winter periods, or in spring.

How to grow: Plant one- or two-year-old divisions, seedlings or rooted cuttings 12in (30cm) apart each way, in moist soil or a prepared bed or bog. Partly bury any trailing stems. In acid soil, dig trenches 9in (23cm) deep and 3ft (90cm) wide and line with heavy-duty polythene. Mix the soil with peat and return to the trench. Firm lightly. Rake in some bonemeal fertilizer. In alkaline soil, fill the trench with a mixture of one part coarse sand to three parts acid peat, or two parts pure acid peat to one part soil. Soak the bed with rainwater before planting. They can also be grown in containers in an ericaceous compost.

Maintenance: Mulch periodically with sawdust or sand. Water regularly, preferably with rainwater. A light dressing of general fertilizer can be applied every two years.

Pruning and training: Cut off some of the sprawling stems and all semi-erect wispy ones in early spring. Apply organic fertilizer if growth is poor.

Propagation: Summer stem cuttings and pegged-down stems root easily. Cranberries can be grown from seed, or divided in autumn.

Harvesting and storing: Pick the berries in autumn when they are fully coloured and beginning to soften. Spread thinly on trays and store in a cool place or a refrigerator for up to two weeks. In temperatures just above freezing and at high humidity they will keep for 2–4 months. Cranberries can also be dried.

Average yields: 4–6lb (1.8–2.7kg) per bush.

Pests and diseases: Few, though in the US the fruit is attacked by various grubs. Lime in the soil or water can cause problems.

Recommended varieties:

(UK/Europe) 'McFarlin' is a late-season variety with large, dark red berries covered in a thick, waxy bloom.

(US) Available varieties include 'Early Black', 'Searless Jumbo', 'Hawes'.

Companion plants: Azaleas, rhododendrons.

ABOVE **Mountain cranberry**

NAME: **CURRANTS – RED AND WHITE**
RIBES SATIVUM
FAMILY: **GROSSULARIACEAE**

Type: Perennial

USDA Zone: 7–8

Description: Red currants have translucent, glossy, red berries with a tart flavour. White currants are colourless with a distinctive grape-like flavour. Both are very productive and attractive enough to be trained into decorative cordons. The plants are self-fertile.

Where to grow: In any reasonable, well-drained neutral to acid (pH6–7) garden soil, but avoid frost pockets. Currants prefer a sunny site if they are to reach their full flavour, but the site can be in semi-shade if it is sheltered.

When to plant: Plant bare-rooted bushes in mid to late autumn or in late winter to early spring. Container–grown plants can be planted at any time if the weather is suitable.

How to grow:

Bush: Dig a hole wide and deep enough to take the fully-extended roots. Cut back to the base any branches less than 6in (15cm) above the previous soil mark. Pull off any suckers. Cut back framework branches to half their length, cutting to an upward-pointing bud. Make sure the previous soil mark is level with the surface of the planting hole before replacing the soil. Tread gently around the base of the plant to firm. Space bushes 5ft (1.5m) apart each way.

Cordon: Dig a hole wide and deep enough to take the fully-extended roots. Insert a cane and attach to a wire support system on a fence or wall. Cut back to the base any branches less than 4in (10cm) above the previous soil mark. Pull out any suckers. Cut back the leader to half its length and tie to the cane. Trim back to a bud all the laterals to 1in (2.5cm) of the main stem. Before replacing the soil, make sure the old soil level is level with the surface. For single cordons, space plants 18in (45cm) apart, and space horizontal wires 24in (60cm) apart, positioning the first wire 4ft (1.2m) from the ground. For double cordons, space plants 3ft (90cm) apart. For triple cordons, space plants 4ft (1.2m) apart. Space rows 5ft (1.5m) apart.

Maintenance: Water regularly in dry weather, particularly when the fruit is beginning to swell. Hand weed. Birds are a problem during winter. Grow currants in a fruit cage or net them. If frosts threaten during flowering cover plants with hessian or netting. When the currants begin to ripen, protect them from birds.

ABOVE **Whitecurrant bush**

Pruning and training:

Bush: In late autumn-early spring, cut back by half any new growth produced by the leaders during the season, and to about 2in (5cm) any side shoots growing from the leaders. Cut out all dead, diseased and crowding wood. In mid-summer, cut back all side shoots on the season's growth four or five leaves from the base.

Cordon: In late winter, prune back the leaders to 6in (15cm) of the current season's growth and all laterals to about 1in (2.5cm) of the main stem. When the top of the cane has been reached, cut back the leader to one bud above the previous season's growth. In early to mid-summer, cut back all side shoots of the current season's growth to four or five leaves from the base. As the leading shoot grows, tie it to the cane.

Propagation: From hardwood cuttings about 12in (30cm) long taken from the current season's growth in mid-autumn. Make a V-shaped trench and put a layer of sand in the bottom. Strip the buds off the lower part of the cutting, leaving four buds at the top, the lowest of which should be 2in (5cm) above the surface. Space the cuttings at a distance of 6in (15cm) apart. Return the soil to the trench. The plants can be dug up during the following autumn when there should be 6in (15cm) of bare stem above the roots.

Harvesting and storing: Currants usually ripen in mid/late summer. Pick when the fruit is ripe in whole clusters, not individually. As the fruits do not all ripen at the same time, several pickings will be necessary. They should be eaten as soon as possible, although they will keep in the refrigerator for about a week.

Average yields: 10lb (4.5kg) per bush. 2–3lb (900g–1.35kg) per single cordon.

Pests and diseases: Birds, aphids – especially the red currant blister aphid – sawfly caterpillars, capsid bugs, leaf spot, coral spot.

Recommended varieties:

Redcurrants: 'Red Lake' (organic) is compact and upright with long trusses of bright red fruit, with a transparent, shiny skin.
'Jonkheer van Tets' (organic) is an early variety with large, juicy berries.

Whitecurrants: 'White Versailles' (organic) has long bunches of very pale yellow fruit borne on large, upright bushes.
'White Hollander' is an upright bush with large, sweet, juicy berries.

Companion plants: Nettles grown nearby, poached egg plant (*Limnanthes douglassii*).

ABOVE **Currant bushes**

NAME: CUSTARD APPLE
ANNONA CHERIMOLA
FAMILY: ANNONACEAE

Type: Tender perennial

USDA zone: 10 (but not cold, winter weather)

Description: The custard apple is an open, sprawling tree about 33ft (10.1m) high. The pale, yellowish-green flowers are borne singly or in clusters, and the medium-green fruit, patterned with scales, turns light green when ripe.

Where to grow: Custard apples prefer dryish, hilly conditions, and a well-drained, slightly acid soil. A sheltered spot in full sun is ideal. They are well worth growing under glass. They also grow well in containers and make lovely pot plants.

When to plant: Bare-rooted plants should be set out in spring or autumn. Container-grown specimens can be planted at any time, provided the weather is suitable.

How to grow: Plant outside 10–25ft (3–7.5m) apart, at the same depth as the original soil mark. Dig a hole wide and deep enough to take the roots when fully extended. Return the soil and water in.

Maintenance: When the young trees start to grow, apply organic fertilizer every four months during their first year. For the best yields of large fruits, hand-pollinate the flowers with a fine brush. Keep weeded and watered, but water less in the winter months to encourage the plants into dormancy.

Pruning and training: Pruning is necessary for the first three or four years to develop well-spaced branches and produce a good framework. Remove a moderate amount of wood each year to keep fruiting branches close to the main stems. Light, annual pruning in late winter/early spring will encourage fruit production. When the tree shape has been formed, no further severe structural pruning should be necessary, but remove any diseased, damaged, dead or crossed branches.

Propagation: By grafting a selected variety on to a seedling rootstock, or from seed.

Harvesting and storing: Harvest when the fruit has grown to its maximum size and changed colour from medium green to a lighter or yellowish green. Mature, firm fruit can be stored at 55°F (13°C), and ripe fruit can be kept in the refrigerator for a few days. Allow the fruit to soften at room temperature. Eat the flesh but not the seeds or skin.

Average yields: A well-grown seven-year-old tree will produce about 100–150 fruits.

Pests and diseases: Citrus mealybug, ants, ambrosia beetle, rust disease.

Recommended varieties:

'Page' crops well, but the fruit tends to split on the tree at maturity.

'Gefner' produces fruit of a good quality.

'Bradley' bears fruit without hand pollination.

Companion plants: None apparent.

ABOVE **Custard apple tree with immature fruit**
INSET **Ripe custard apples**

NAME: **DAMSON**
PRUNUS INSITITIA
FAMILY: **ROSACEAE**

Type: Perennial

USDA zone: 5–9

Description: The damson grows to a height of 12–15ft (3.6-4.5m). It flowers in mid-spring and the fruits ripen in mid-autumn. Most damsons are self-compatible, but planting suitable pollinators nearby will ensure better cropping.

Where to grow: Damsons enjoy a deep, moisture-retentive, well-drained soil (pH6.5–7). They will tolerate some shade and can be grown against an east-facing wall or fence.

When to plant: Late autumn to early spring, 10–12ft (3–3.6m) apart. Plant container-grown plants at any time if the weather is suitable. The most suitable rootstocks are the semi-dwarfing 'St Julien A' and the dwarfing 'Pixy'.

How to grow:

Bush, half standard and standard trees: Buy partly-trained 2–3 year old plants. Prepare the ground in early autumn and fork in a balanced organic fertilizer just before planting. Dig a hole wide and deep enough to take the fully extended roots. Before planting trees in the open, drive in a stake.

Fan-trained specimens: Construct a system of horizontal wires 6in (15cm) apart. Plant the trees to the same depth as in the nursery, back-fill with soil and firm. Tie to the stake with a tree tie, or tie in the branches of the fan to the wire support system. Water in well.

Maintenance: Hoe to keep weed-free and water regularly in dry weather. Apply a balanced organic fertilizer in late winter. Protect fruit grown on walls and fences against frost by draping with netting or hessian. Thin fruitlets in early summer if necessary, using scissors.

Pruning and training:

Bush, half-standard and standard: During late winter/early spring of the second year, select four branches that are wide-angled to the stem and cut back each leader by half to an outward-facing bud. Remove the remainder, including the lower laterals. In summer, remove shoots on main stem below the head, and any suckers that have grown from the ground. In the third year, repeat the previous year's procedures, but let more secondary branches (up to 8) develop. From late winter-early spring cut back the maiden growth of these strong branches by half, to outward-facing buds. Prune back to 3–4in (7.5–10cm) any unpruned laterals on the inside of the tree. In subsequent years, little pruning or training will be necessary.

Fans: Prune only in spring and summer. In the spring of the second year, to encourage new shoots, cut back the two side shoots tied to canes at a 45° angle to a triple bud 12–18in (30–45cm) from the main stem. In summer, select four strong shoots from each arm, one on the lower side of the branch, two equally spaced on the upper side, and one to extend the existing rib, making a total of eight by the end of the growing season. Pinch back all developing shoots to one leaf. Train each new shoot to a cane to extend the fan wings, keeping the centre open. In the third year, cut each leader by a third, to a downward-pointing bud, in early spring. In summer, let each leading shoot on the eight ribs extend. Select three more shoots on each branch and train them outwards, tying them to canes attached to the wires. Rub out any buds growing towards the structure. On the upper and lower sides of the ribs, allow young shoots to grow at a distance of 4in (10cm) apart. Pinch any surplus shoots back to one leaf. Repeat as necessary. When the selected laterals reach about 18in (45cm), pinch out the growing points unless they are needed for the framework. In late summer, tie them to canes attached to the wires. They will bear fruit the following summer. In subsequent years, the wire structure should be covered with framework branches with fruit-bearing laterals 4in (10cm) apart. Pruning is now aimed at the annual renewal of new shoots, so cut out shoots that have borne fruit to make way for new ones. In late spring, remove shoots growing towards and away from the wall or fence, leaving two leaves on shoots with flower buds at the base. The previous summer's laterals will be carrying blossom and side shoots. Choose one side shoot at the base as a replacement, one in the middle as a reserve, and one at the tip to extend the lateral. Pinch back remaining side shoots to two leaves. Pinch out the growing points of the basal side shoot and reserve lateral when 18in (45cm) long and of the fruit-carrying extension later on when it has six leaves.

Propagation: By budding or grafting, usually done at the nursery.

Harvesting and storing: Pick fruits for bottling or making jam when they are slightly under-ripe. Pick with the stalks intact. Fruits do not ripen simultaneously, so it will be necessary to pick several times. The fruit will keep for a couple of weeks in a cool place.

Average yields: Bush, half-standard and standard; 30–60lb (13.6–27kg) per tree. Fans; 15–25lb (7–11.3kg) per fan.

Pests and diseases: Aphids, honey fungus, powdery mildew, leaf spot. Birds may attack the fruit buds.

Recommended varieties:

'Merryweather' (organic) is a self-fertile, vigorous variety that produces large, firm, juicy damsons. 'Farleigh Damson' is a fast-growing variety that makes a good windbreak.

'Prune' or 'Shropshire Damson' (organic) is a self-fertile variety of dwarfish growth that bears small, oval, blue-black fruits of excellent flavour.

Companion plants: Garlic, horseradish and borage.

ABOVE **Damsons crop heavily and are excellent for jam**

111

NAME: **FIG**
FICUS CARICA
FAMILY: **MORACEAE**

Type: Perennial

USDA zone: 9–10

Description: Figs have pear-shaped, brown-green fruits and large, distinctive leaves. They can be grown as trees or bushes and thrive in hot, dry climates. Almost all figs set their fruit parthenocarpically (without fertilization).

Where to grow: Figs like well-drained, deep, rich, moisture-retentive soil (pH 6.5–7) and a warm, sunny position. A south-facing wall is ideal. Cool, wet conditions may induce too much growth and poorer crops. They can also be grown in pots. In cool areas, fan-trained figs can be grown under glass.

When to plant: Late autumn until early spring.

How to grow: For a fig pit, dig a hole 24 x 24 x 24in (60 x 60 x 60cm). Line the sides with paving slabs and place a 9–10in (23–25cm) layer of bricks at the bottom. Plant the tree, spreading the roots well. Fill with mixed soil and bonemeal, to which a little rubble may be added. If grown against a wall, plant 9in (23cm) away.

ABOVE **Young figs developing on a tree**

Maintenance: Water well in hot, dry weather. Water pot-grown figs regularly and repot and root-prune every 2–3 years in winter. Apply a well-rotted manure mulch in spring and an organic fertilizer where roots are restricted. In summer, feed occasionally with diluted liquid feeds, but do not overfeed. In late autumn, cover the tender parts with straw to protect the young shoots and embryo fruits of both outside trees and those under glass. Tie loosely in place and remove gradually in mid-late spring. Move pot-grown plants under cover.

Propagation: From cuttings taken from well-ripened wood. Take 12in (30cm) long sections and bury 6in (15cm) deep in a sheltered, sunny spot in a well-drained soil. Transplant to their growing positions after two years

Pruning and training: Prune established bushes and fans in early summer. Pinch back all young shoots to five leaves and tie to the wires if fan-trained. Thin fruits in early autumn, keeping the small fruits close to the end of the shoots which are next year's harvest.

Harvesting and storing: Figs are usually ready in late summer/autumn, when the fully-coloured fruits begin to droop, the skin begins to crack, and a drop of nectar is seen at the base. Pick carefully and store in a cool place for several weeks. Remove small fruit that will not ripen.

Average yields: Bush, 12–50lb (5.4–23kg); fan, 5–25lb (900g–11.3kg), depending on the age of the tree and the weather.

Pests and diseases: Birds, wasps, canker, grey mould (botrytis).

Recommended varieties:

'Brunswick' has well-flavoured oval fruit.

'Brown Turkey' is a heavy cropper with rich, red flesh and a sweet flavour, and can be grown outdoors or under glass.

'White Marseilles' has pear-shaped fruit, whitish, almost transparent flesh and is good for container growing.

Companion plants: Rue.

NAME: **GOOSEBERRY**
RIBES UVA-CRISPA
FAMILY: **GROSSULARIACEAE**

Type: Hardy perennial

USDA zone: 6–8

Description: Gooseberries are green, red, white or yellow. All gooseberry cultivars are self-fertile, and the plants need cool conditions to succeed.

Where to grow: Gooseberries prefer a well-drained medium slightly acid (pH 6) loam. They grow best in an open, sunny position that is sheltered from strong winds.

When to plant: Plant bare-rooted bushes in mid-late autumn or late winter to early spring. Plant container-grown plants at any time if the weather is suitable.

How to grow: Space bush varieties 5ft (1.5m) apart, single cordons 18in (45cm) apart, double cordons 24in (60cm) apart, and triple cordons 3ft (90cm) apart. Space rows 5ft (1.5m) apart.

Bushes: Pull off any suckers and cut back to the base any branches less than 6in (15cm) above the old soil mark. Dig a hole wide and deep enough to take the roots when fully extended. Make sure that the original soil mark is level with the ground, spread out the roots and replace the soil. Tread the plants in gently. Cut the framework branches to half their length, cutting to an upward pointing bud.

Cordons: Dig a hole, insert a cane and attach it to horizontal wires placed at 4ft (1.2m) from the ground and 2ft (60cm) apart along a fence or wall. Pull out any suckers. Cut back to the base any branches less than 4in (10cm) above the original soil mark. Cut back the leader by half and tie it to the cane. Trim back the laterals to a bud, about 1in (2.5cm) from the main stem. Make sure the original soil mark is level with the ground and infill with soil. Tread the plants in gently. Tie the cane to the wires.

Maintenance: Gooseberries, like most fruit bushes, have shallow roots and should be weeded carefully. They flower in mid-spring so protect from frost and birds. For large berries, thin by removing alternate fruit in late spring. If you prefer small or medium fruit do not thin. Net the bushes when the fruits begin to ripen and again in winter. Mulch with well-rotted manure or compost in early spring . Remove any suckers sprouting around the base. Water newly planted bushes in summer if the weather is dry, and feed the plants in winter with an organic, potash fertilizer.

Pruning: Young plants can be trained as bushes, cordons or fans.

Bushes: In winter of the first year, prune all the shoots by about half to an outward-facing bud.

Established bushes: To prevent overcrowding and retain an open centre, cut out older branches in winter.

Spurs: Prune new side shoots to a bud about 3in (7.5cm) from their base. Prune branch leaders to three–four buds of the new growth.

Cordons: In late winter prune back the leaders to about 6in (15cm) of the current season's

ABOVE **A newly-planted gooseberry bush**

growth. Cut back all laterals to around 1in (2.5cm) of the main stem. When the cordons have reached the top of the cane, cut back the leader to one bud above the previous season's growth. In early summer, cut back all side shoots produced by the current season's growth to four or five leaves from the base. Tie the leading shoot to the cane as it grows.

Propagation: Take hardwood cuttings 12in (30cm) long from the current season's well-ripened wood in early autumn. Make a straight cut at the bottom, and a sloping one at the top. Using a spade, make a V-shaped trench and put a layer of sand at the bottom. Strip off the buds, leaving four at the top. Plant the cuttings 6in (15cm) apart with the lowest four buds 2in (5cm) above the soil's surface. Infill with soil. Leave the cuttings in situ until the following autumn and then lift and replant, exposing more of the stem.

Harvesting and storing: Pick when the fruit is fully coloured, soft when squeezed gently, and detaches easily from the stalk. The fruit will not ripen at the same time, so will need to be harvested several times. Gooseberries are best eaten fresh, but will keep in a refrigerator for 10 days–two weeks. They can be frozen.

Average yields: 10lb (4.5kg) per bush; 2–3lb (900g–1.35kg) per cordon.

Pests and diseases: Birds, sawfly larvae, powdery mildew, bacterial or fungal leaf spots.

Recommended varieties:

'Greenfinch' (organic) is a mildew resistant, compact plant that produces high yields of smooth skinned fruit.

'Invicta' (organic) is a late-ripening red dessert gooseberry with large fruit.

'Martlett (Red)' (organic) is a late-ripening, red dessert gooseberry with large fruit.

Companion plants: Roses, broad beans, tomatoes, strawberries, poached egg plant.

NAME: **GRAPE – DESSERT**
VITIS VINIFERA
FAMILY: **VITACEAE**

Type: Hardy perennial

USDA Zone: 9–10 (also 8 in a warm, sheltered position).

Description: The grape vine is a deciduous climber with heart-shaped leaves, insignificant sweetly perfumed, white flowers and dark red or green grapes.

Where to grow: Grapes grow in most soils apart from chalk and clay, if drainage is good. They like gritty or sandy soil (pH6.5–7) with plenty of organic matter incorporated. They can be grown outdoors, trained over an arbour or pergola, as a shaded roof over a terrace, and in large containers. A wider selection can be grown in the warmth of the greenhouse.

When to plant: Mid to late autumn or late winter to early spring. Early spring is the best time to plant outdoors. Winter planted varieties will need a 4in (10cm) layer of leaf mould around them. Container-grown specimens can be planted at any time of the year.

How to grow outdoors: Choose a wall that faces south, south-east or south-west. Four to six weeks before planting, dig a hole 24–30in (60–75cm) deep and wide for each planting position, incorporating organic matter. Return the soil and scatter organic fertilizer over the surface. Construct a support system with the wires starting 18in (45cm) from the ground and 12in (30cm) apart. Secure with vine eyes, 9in (23cm) away from the wall. Insert a cane, then plant the one-year-old vine to the depth of the original soil mark. Space plants 5ft (1.5m) apart. Firm in. Cut back the main shoot or 'rod' to 24in (60cm), and tie to the cane support. Prune all side shoots to one bud.

How to grow in the greenhouse: Plant the vine outside and bring the shoot or 'rod' through a hole in the floor, or plant in the greenhouse border. Plant in late autumn to early winter if possible. Add coarse grit and organic matter to the soil to prepare the bed. Erect a support system as for outside grown grapes, placing the wires at 9in (23cm) intervals. Finish 18in (45cm) below the ridge. Leave 15–18in (37.5–45cm) between the wires and glass to prevent scorching. Train the rod up towards the greenhouse ride, parallel with the glass. Alternatively, plant near a corner and run the rod horizontally along the side wall and train the laterals vertically from it.

Maintenance outdoors: In early spring, apply an organic fertilizer, water the surface of the soil and spread a 2in (5cm) mulch of well-rotted manure. In hot, dry conditions water regularly. From fruit formation until colouring, feed dessert grapes with liquid organic fertilizer high in potash. Thinning may be necessary. Protect the plants from birds once the fruit begins to ripen. Netting can be used.

Maintenance under glass: In late winter/early spring soak the greenhouse bed with water and mulch with well-rotted manure. Damp down and water every week during hot spells, gradually reducing the watering as the grapes ripen. Avoid rapid rises of temperature. When growth begins, apply a potash liquid feed every two weeks. This should then be done on a weekly basis when the vine flowers, and then stopped when the fruit begins to colour. After harvesting from early autumn onwards, cut back the laterals by one half. Pinch out the growing point when the rod reaches the ridge of the greenhouse. Prune back to 1in (2.5cm) of new growth in early winter and cut back all the laterals produced in the previous summer to one bud. Keep the top about 15in (37.5cm) from the ridge. Hand pollination will be necessary once the flowers are open. From early summer, thin the grapes over a period of a week using long-bladed scissors.

Pruning and training: The Guyot system is usually used outdoors, but cordons can be used for both outdoor and greenhouse vines. In spring and summer of the first and second years, train the leader up the cane and tie loosely. Train laterals alternately to the right and left of the leader onto the wires, cut them back to five leaves, and remove the flowers. In late autumn to early winter, cut by half the new growth made by the leader. To form the fruiting spurs, cut back the laterals to 1in (2.5cm) from the leader. In the third and subsequent years, repeat the first and second year pruning, but when the tree begins to flower in spring cut back the fruiting lateral to two leaves beyond the truss and prune back sub-laterals to one leaf. Keep one fruiting lateral per

ABOVE **Grapes growing on a vine**

spur and rub out the others. Leave one bunch of grapes per lateral for the first few years. A mature vine will support two or three bunches on one lateral. In late autumn to early winter cut back by half the leader's new growth. When the top support wire has been reached, cut it back to 1in (2.5cm) beyond the previous season's growth.

Propagation: By grafting or by 8in (20cm) hardwood cuttings taken in winter and inserted 6in (15cm) deep in sandy soil.

Harvesting and storing: The vine will fruit three years after planting. Remove some of the foliage or tie it back to allow the sun to reach the ripening fruit. Cut ripe bunches with a short piece of woody stem or 'handle' attached. Handle carefully so that the bloom is not spoiled or the fruit damaged. Store the fruit for up to two weeks at room temperature, with the 'handle' in a narrow-necked jar of water.

Average yields: About 15lb (7kg) of fruit from a mature grapevine.

Pests and diseases: Scale insects, vine weevils, wasps, downy mildew, botrytis.

Recommended varieties:

'Black Hamburgh' (organic) is a black dessert grape with blue-black skin that is suitable for growing outside or in the greenhouse.

'Leon Millot' (organic) is a vigorous black grape suitable for dessert and wine making. It is a reliable cropper with good resistance to mildew.

'Fragola' (organic) produces pinkish-red grapes that taste of wood strawberries and gives good autumn colour.

Companion plants: Blackberries, mustard, sage, hyssop, mulberries.

NAME: **GRAPEFRUIT**
CITRUS X PARADISI
FAMILY: **RUTACEAE**

Type: Tender evergreen

USDA zone: 8–10

Description: The grapefruit tree is a glossy-leaved, fast-growing, spreading evergreen with star-shaped flowers. It is thought to be a cross between an orange and a pomelo. Fruits have light yellow, slightly acidic flesh and grow in large, grape-like clusters. They can take up to a year to ripen. Most citrus fruits are self-fertile.

Where to grow: The grapefruit tolerates a wide range of soils, but a fertile, well-drained, slightly acidic soil (pH6.5) is ideal. It likes a sunny site sheltered from winds. A south-facing wall is ideal as the reflected heat helps to sweeten the fruit. In cooler climates, grow in containers, which look good on the patio.

When to plant: Transplant pot-grown trees into larger containers in winter. In cooler climates, the fruits should be under glass during frosty months when they flower and fruit.

How to grow:

Outdoors: Plant 15–30ft (5–10m) apart each way, depending on the cultivar.

Under glass: Plant in containers at least 24in (60cm) in diameter, filled with a nutrient-rich compost. Overwinter at 50–54°F (10–12°C).

Maintenance: Water outside trees frequently until established. In mid-summer, water every ten days and mulch to conserve moisture. Apply organic fertilizer every month from late winter until late summer. Protect from frost.

Under glass: Scrape 2in (5cm) of compost off the top of the pot of container-grown trees in mid-spring, and replace with new compost. Maintain a minimum temperature of 68°F (20°C) with 75 per cent humidity. Water regularly and give a liquid organic fertilizer once a month. Put container-grown trees outside in summer if the weather is good.

ABOVE **Huge, ripe grapefruit ready for harvesting**

Pruning and training: In late winter, cut the main branches of newly-planted trees by a third to encourage lateral growth. Remove crossed, dead or diseased branches after harvesting. Prune to retain the shape of the tree.

Propagation: By T-budding, cuttings or seed.

Harvesting and storing: Harvest the fruit when ripe, usually from late autumn to early spring.

Average yields: 20–30 fruits may be picked from a well-grown tree, depending on its age and size.

Pests and diseases: Sooty mould, red spider mite, whitefly, greenfly, scale insects. Spraying with soapy water will help the problem.

Recommended varieties:

'Golden Special' is a well-branched tree that has glossy leaves.

'Marsh's Seedless' is the most common variety, and has greenish-white flesh.

'Duncan' is a pink-fleshed variety.

Companion plants: Oak and guava trees.

NAME: GUAVA
PSIDIUM GUAJAVA
FAMILY: MYRTACEAE

Type: Perennial
USDA zone: 10
Description: Guavas have leathery leaves and green fruits that ripen to yellow or red. They have a strong, musky smell and tart white or pink flesh, surrounded by hard, round seeds. Guavas are partly self-fertile, but growing two or more cultivars may increase yields.
Where to grow: Guavas can be grown in a sunny, sheltered position outdoors. They enjoy well-drained soil rich in organic matter (pH6).
When to plant: Set out container-grown plants at any time, if the weather is suitable.
How to grow: Plant outdoors 15ft (4.5m) apart each way. In exposed areas, stake the young trees securely and erect a windbreak if necessary. Guavas can also be grown under cover in greenhouse border beds or containers 12–14in (30–35cm) in diameter. Use a rich compost with a little organic fertilizer added. Maintain a temperature of 72°F (22°C) with 70 per cent humidity. Hand-pollination may be necessary. Keep the atmosphere dry during the flowering period.
Maintenance: Top-dress with organic fertilizer two or three times during the growing season. Water well and apply a mulch of well-rotted manure to conserve moisture. Weed round the bases of the trees. Plants grown in greenhouse containers can be put outdoors in summer.
Pruning and training: Encourage branching by cutting back the leading shoot to about a third of its length when the tree is about 3ft (90cm) tall. Prune to stimulate new growth and keep the fruits close to the centre of the plant. Remove any crossing, dead or diseased branches and any low ones that touch the soil.

ABOVE **Guava**

Propagation: From seed-sown trays or 3in (7.5cm) pots of rich compost. Germination will take two–three weeks. Pot on the strongest plants into 6in (15cm) pots when they are around 8in (20cm) tall. Harden off and transplant when they are 12in (30cm) high. Certain cultivars can be chip-budded. Guavas can be propagated by 5–6in (12.5–15cm) softwood cuttings in spring. Outdoors, they can be increased by layering and from suckers dug from round the base of the tree.

Harvesting and storing: Tropical guavas turn yellow when ripe. Grown outdoors, they may produce fruit after one–three years, depending on the cultivar. The fruits ripen about five months after fertilization and can be stored for around a month at a temperature of just below 50°F (10 °C).

Average yields: A four-year-old tree can produce 30 fruits, depending on cultivar, age of plant and season of cropping.

Pests and diseases: Outdoor trees can suffer from aphids, fruit flies and scale insects. Plants under glass can be plagued by whitefly and thrips. Seedlings may suffer from damping off.

Recommended varieties:
'Miami White' has white flesh.
'Malherbe' has pink flesh.

Companion plants: Citrus fruit trees.

NAME: KIWI FRUIT
ACTINIDIA CHINENSIS/DELICIOSA
FAMILY: ACTINIDIACEAE

Type: Perennial
USDA zone: 9–10
Description: Kiwi fruit or Chinese gooseberry is a trailing climber. The hairy, brown-skinned fruits have green pulp and small, black seeds. Modern varieties are self-fertile.

Where to grow: Kiwi fruit prefer well-drained, deep sandy soil (pH7) with organic matter incorporated. They need long, warm summers to succeed, and like a hot, sunny position – a sunny wall is perfect. They are rampant climbers and will reach 30ft (9m) if unchecked. In cold areas, cover to protect from frost; a walk-in polytunnel is useful as they are too vigorous for the average greenhouse.

When to plant: Mid-autumn to early spring. Early spring is the best time to plant outdoors.

How to grow: Plant 15ft (4.5m) apart, or use pots 12in (30cm) in depth and diameter and soak for an hour before planting. Tease out the roots gently and plant to the same depth as before. Firm in well and water. In spring, top the pot with a 1in (2.5cm) layer of well-rotted manure. Insert canes in the pot and drape with

ABOVE **Sliced kiwi fruit**

netting or horticultural fleece to protect the blossom from frost. To plant outside dig a hole deep and wide enough to take the spread roots. Plant 9in (23cm) from a wall with a trellis or a system of wires attached. Position the plant and tease out the roots. Replace the soil and firm. Once planted prune to 12in (30cm) high. When the plant has covered the available space, pinch out the growing point.

Maintenance: Water regularly and keep weed free. Apply a heavy mulch and potassium-rich fertilizer in spring. Thinning is rarely necessary.

Pruning and training: In the first and second years, cut back all fruited side shoots to 2–4 buds during the dormant period. In early summer, prune the young plant to just above the top of the support. In summer, train along wires stopping any laterals at five leaves when the space is filled. In the growing season of the third year, pinch back the young fruit to seven leaves beyond the last fruit. In winter, cut back the lateral to two buds beyond where the last fruit was set.

Propagation: In spring, take softwood cuttings 4–6in (10–15cm) long, and insert in compost. In late summer, take hardwood cuttings 8–12in (20–30cm) long and insert in sandy compost. Whip-and-tongue grafting and T-budding can also be used.

Harvesting and storing: Kiwi fruits begin to fruit 3–4 years after planting. Harvest as they soften by snapping from the branch with the calyx attached. They will keep for several months at 32°F (0°C) wrapped in plastic film.

Average yields: About 20lb (9kg) of fruit from a mature seven-year-old plant.

Pests and diseases: Dieback in winter.

Recommended varieties:

'Jenny' and 'Oriental Delight' are self-fertile. 'Blake' is a high-yielding self-fertile variety.

Companion plants: None known.

NAME: **KUMQUAT** *FORTUNELLA JAPONICA/F. MARGARITA* FAMILY: **RUTACEAE**

Type: Evergreen

USDA zone: 9–10

Description: Kumquat trees are small, frost tender evergreens that reach a height of around 10ft (3m). They have attractive, shiny leaves and sweetly scented, white flowers that appear in summer. The fruits are small and yellow, like miniature oranges.

Where to grow: Kumquats prefer well-drained, medium-heavy, slightly acid soil (pH6–6.5) and an open position in full sun. Incorporate plenty of organic matter to aid water retention. Kumquats can be grown in pots in a heated greenhouse in temperate regions, and outdoors in temperatures above 15°F (–10°C). They are often grown as ornamental plants.

When to plant: Plant container-grown plants at any time, if the weather is suitable. Set out bare-rooted trees in late spring/early summer, when all danger of frost has passed, or autumn.

How to grow: Space 8–12ft (2.4–3.6m) apart, or in hedged rows 12ft (3.6m) apart. If pot-grown use a dwarf cultivar and a pot 18in (45cm) in diameter. Sow ripe seed in trays in the greenhouse and prick out the seedlings into individual pots. Grow them on in the greenhouse for their first two winters.

Maintenance: Keep weed free, apply regular feeds, and mulch with well-rotted manure. Water the plants well while the fruits are swelling. Protect trees outdoors from frost during winter. Pots can be put out in summer, but require cool, sunny conditions under glass in winter. Re-pot container-grown plants annually.

Pruning and training: Thin out crowded branches. Prune fruited shoots after harvesting.

Propagation: Kumquats are rarely grown from seed because they do not do well on their own rootstocks. Propagation is usually by grafting on to the trifoliate orange rootstock *Poncirus trifoliate*, which dwarfs the tree, or on to grapefruit or sour orange rootstocks.

Harvesting and storing: The trees crop from 7–8 years. Pick the fruit when fully coloured. Its thick peel gives the kumquat good handling qualities. It can be stored in the refrigerator for up to a week, and the fruit can be preserved in brandy and made into preserves.

Average yields: Up to 5 fruits per shoot.

Pests and diseases: Mealybugs, whitefly, red spider mite, gall wasp, aphids, scale insects, lemon scab.

Recommended varieties:

'Fucushii' is a weeping, bushy variety that bears large, oval fruits.

'Meiwa' is a dwarf tree, often thornless, with orange-yellow fruits.

'Nagami' is widely cultivated in America. It fruits from mid-autumn to mid-winter.

Companion plants: Rubber, oak and guava trees growing nearby.

ABOVE **Kumquats growing on a tree**
INSET **Harvested kumquats**

NAME: **LEMON**
CITRUS LIMON
FAMILY: **RUTACEAE**

Type: Tender evergreen

USDA zone: 8–10

Description: The lemon is a decorative plant with glossy, evergreen leaves, scented purple tinged white flowers and large yellow fruits. Trees can reach a height of 10–30ft (3–9m).

Where to grow: Lemons like a sheltered, sunny spot. They do well in fertile, well-drained slightly acid soils (pH 6–6.5) and can be grown under glass. Outdoors, they need a temperature of 68°F (20°C). Compact cultivars like Meyer's lemon (*Citrus x meyeri* 'Meyeri') are ideal for containers. They crop at 7–8 years old and fruit all year because they can take from 6–8 months from fruit set to ripen, depending on climate.

When to plant: The best time to plant outside is spring or autumn. Plant container-grown plants at any time if the weather is suitable.

How to grow: Maintain a temperature of 59–86°F (15–30°C) for best results. Under glass, plant in prepared border beds or containers 24in (60cm) in diameter, filled with a rich compost. Maintain a minimum temperature of 68°F (20°C) with 75 per cent humidity. Outdoors, plant from 15–30ft (4.5–9m) each way depending on the vigour of the cultivar.

Maintenance: During the first few years, feed with a high-nitrogen fertilizer during the growing season. Spray with seaweed solution every week. Weed carefully and water well in dry spells, especially when the flowers or fruit are developing. Thinning is unnecessary.

Pruning and training: In the first year, shorten by a third the main branches of newly-planted trees to produce a rounded shape. Remove dead, diseased or crossing branches after fruiting. Trees can be trained as standards or half standards, but these may be too big for an average garden.

Propagation: Commercial plants are grafted or budded. Also from seed or cuttings.

Harvesting and storing: When ripe, cut with secateurs. Store in layers in sand in a paper-lined, wooden box, in a cool place for up to two months.

Average yields: One tree may yield more than 500 fruits every winter.

Pests and diseases: Mealy bugs, scale insects, red spider mite, aphids, gall wasp, root and crown rots, lemon scab.

Recommended varieties:

'Eureka' is medium size, almost thornless and prolific, and the fruit is elliptic to oblong.

'Lisbon' is large, vigorous, thorny and prolific, and the fruit is yellow and faintly pitted.

'Villa Franca' is more vigorous, thorny, larger and has denser foliage than 'Eureka'.

Companion plants: In warm countries, lemons are grown near rubber, oak and guava trees.

ABOVE **Lemons ripening on a tree**

NAME: **LOGANBERRY/TAYBERRY/ BOYSENBERRY**
RUBUS HYBRID
FAMILY: **ROSACEAE**

Type: Perennial

USDA zone: 8–9

Description: These berries are crosses between different *Rubus* species or cultivars. Fruit is borne on canes from mid-summer until the first frosts. Hybrid berries crop after 1–2 years.

Where to grow: The berries need a medium, deep loam, fertile and well-drained (pH7) and thrive in full sun, but will tolerate partial shade.

When to plant: Late winter to early spring.

How to grow: Stretch wires across fences, trellises and walls, or use a post and wire system. Dig planting stations 24in (60cm) deep and wide in autumn/early winter, 8ft (2.4m) apart for tayberries and 15ft (4.5m) apart for loganberries and boysenberries. Fork in 3in (7.5cm) of well-rotted manure. Refill with a mixture of soil and well-rotted compost and dress with bonemeal. Plant bare-rooted canes at the original soil depth. Cut down each cane to 6–8in (15–20cm).

Maintenance: Hand weed or shallow hoe. Water in summer if the weather is dry. Dress with an organic fertilizer, water in, then mulch with well-rotted manure in early spring.

Pruning and training: Common methods are fan, weaving and roping. For fans, train fruiting canes individually to left and right and new canes centrally. To weave, tie canes to the support in summer and weave in and out of the lower three wires. In the second summer, train new canes up through the centre of the bush and along the top wire. After fruiting, cut out all fruited canes to the base and weave the current season's canes around the lower three wires. Remove weak tips. For roping, train all shoots to one side of the support in the first year. As they

ABOVE **Thornless loganberry**

grow, train to the other side. Subsequently, cut out canes that have borne fruit in autumn and tie 3–4 new canes horizontally along each wire.

Propagation: Tip-layer in summer and sever the new plant from the parent in autumn/early winter. They will not come true from seed.

Harvesting and storing: Pick by twisting slightly when soft and fully coloured. Eat fresh or freeze.

Average yields: 10–30lb (4.5–13.5kg) per established plant, depending on size/variety.

Pests and diseases: Birds, aphids, raspberry beetle, botrytis, various virus diseases, spur blight, cane spot.

Recommended varieties:

Loganberry: 'LY59' is a heavy cropper that is quite thorny with long, sharp-tasting fruits. 'LY654' is a less-vigorous, thornless variety.

Tayberry: Medana type is resistant to virus and has fruits larger and sweeter than loganberries.

Boysenberry: The thornless variety is easier to handle, but not as good a cropper.

Companion plants: Marigolds, tansy, chives.

NAME: **LOQUAT**
ERIOBOTRYA JAPONICA
FAMILY: **ROSACEAE**

Type: Evergreen

USDA zone: 8–10

Description: Loquat trees are dense evergreens with large, leathery leaves and fragrant, yellowish flowers in autumn. The round, oval, or pear-shaped fruits ripen in late winter and spring and are yellow with scented, white pulp. The plants need a minimum temperature of 59°F (15°C) to fruit regularly. Most cultivars are self-fertile, but may also be pollinated by insects. Loquats are dense evergreens, so plants cannot be grown underneath them.

Where to grow: Loquats prefer a fertile, well-drained soil and a warm, sunny situation. They grow well on warm walls, but in temperate climates will only fruit under glass. They can be grown in large pots.

ABOVE **Loquats have juicy, scented white pulp**

When to plant: Set out container-grown plants at any time if the weather is suitable.

How to grow:

Outside: Plant loquats 12–15ft (3.6–4.5m) apart each way.

Under glass: Set out seed-raised plants about 18in (45cm) high in prepared beds or large containers. Maintain a minimum temperature of 64°F (18°C).

Maintenance: Keep the surrounding area weed-free and apply organic fertilizer every three or four months. Water well in dry weather and mulch with organic matter to preserve moisture. Thin during the early stages of development so that the fruitlets are evenly spaced.

Pruning and training: Remove dead, diseased, or damaged branches. Shorten additional stems to let in light. Tip-prune over-vigorous shoots.

Propagation: From fresh seed, T-budding on rootstocks including hawthorn and quince, by air layering or by softwood cuttings.

Harvesting and storing: The fruits ripen in late winter/early spring. Harvest when they begin to soften and turn yellow or orange. They can be stored for a short time at 41–50°F (5–10°C).

Average yields: An average tree can produce around 110lb (50kg) of fruit in the right conditions, depending on where it is grown.

Pests and diseases: Little trouble when grown outdoors. Under glass can be prone to attack by mealybugs, thrips, whitefly and red spider mite.

Recommended varieties:

'Big Jim' ripens in mid season and bears large, pale-orange, round to oblong fruit.

'Mrs Cooksey' is a New Zealand variety that has large fruit with well-flavoured, yellow flesh.

'Vista White' bears small to medium size fruit with light yellow skin and pure white flesh.

'Benlehr' produces medium-sized, oval to oblong fruit with thin skin and white, juicy flesh.

Companion plants: None known.

NAME: **MANGO**
MANGIFERA INDICA
FAMILY: **ANACARDIACEAE**

Type: Evergreen

USDA zone: 10

Description: The mango is a self-fertile, medium to large tree with dark green, long, narrow foliage. The large, colourful fruit has tough skin and a huge, flat stone. Trees raised from seed bear fruit at 5–7 years old. Budded or grafted stock bears fruit 3–4 years after planting.

Where to grow: Mangos like a deep, well-drained soil (pH 5.5–7.5) and a warm, sunny site protected from strong winds. They do well in both medium clay and sandy loam soils. Grow also under glass and in containers. Low humidity can cause fruit drop and leaf scorch.

When to plant: Plant out container-grown trees at any time, if the weather is suitable.

How to grow: Dwarfing rootstocks are more suitable for smaller gardens. Plant 25ft (7.5m) apart each way, or 30–40ft for more vigorous cultivars. To grow from seed, soak the seed for 48 hours. Plant in a compost-filled pot with the hump at soil level. Seeds do best with bottom heat and usually germinate in 2–4 weeks.

Under glass: Mangos grown from seed may be too vigorous to grow under glass unless on dwarfing rootstocks. Transplant young plants about 3ft (90cm) high, into prepared beds or containers. Maintain a minimum temperature of 70–77°F (21–25°C) with 75 per cent humidity. In temperate areas, flowering usually takes place at the end of the growing season.

Maintenance: Under glass, water plants regularly and liquid feed every four weeks. If the leaves turn yellow, spray with a nitrogenous fertilizer. Outside, apply a general fertilizer three or four times a year during the growing season.

ABOVE **A mango ripening on a tree**

Water well in dry weather, particularly in the first few years when the roots are developing. Mulch to retain moisture and suppress weeds, and thin fruits during years of good production.

Pruning and training: Prune the leading shoot when it is 3ft (90cm) long to encourage lateral branching. Remove dead, diseased and damaged branches. Remove overcrowded growth in the early years to ensure a rounded, evenly-spaced framework.

Propagation: Veneer/ side veneer grafting and chip budding are the most successful methods. From seed, polyembryonic types (with seeds containing more than one embryo) generally come true. Monoembryonic (single embryo) types do not, so graft them on to seedling rootstocks.

Harvesting and storing: Mangos taste best if left to ripen on the tree. Cut when they change colour and begin to soften. Store for 2–4 weeks at 48°F (9°C) with 90–95 per cent humidity.

Average yields: A 10–20 year-old tree can produce 200–300 fruits. At twice that age and over, the yield will be doubled.

Pests and diseases: In the tropics, fruit flies, mealybugs and scale insects. In temperate regions, trees grown outside may be affected by anthracnose and powdery mildew. Plants under glass can suffer from aphids, whitefly, thrips, red spider mite and powdery and downy mildew.

Recommended varieties:
'Brooks' is a somewhat dwarfing tree suitable for the greenhouse and containers. It bears medium to large, kidney-shaped, yellow fruit with a light green blush.
'Sensation' is broad and rounded, and the fruit is small and yellow with a red blush.
'Tommy Atkins' bears large, orange-yellow, thick skinned fruit. It is resistant to anthracnose.

Companion plants: None apparent.

NAME: MEDLAR
MESPILUS GERMANICA
FAMILY: ROSACEAE

Type: Perennial

USDA zone: 4–7

Description: Medlars are self-fertile with leathery leaves, single large white flowers and brownish-green fruits about the size of an apple. The seed chambers are visible through the open cup below the calyx.

Where to grow: Medlars grow in most soils, except badly drained and chalky ones. They prefer a sunny, sheltered site, but will tolerate partial shade. They are good in containers and ideal for the ornamental garden, or as a specimen plant in a lawn.

When to plant: Late autumn/winter is best.

How to grow: Medlars are usually supplied as two or three-year-old standards or as half standards. Prepare the ground in the autumn before planting. Dig out a hole wide and deep enough to take the roots of the tree when fully extended, and drive in a stake. Plant to the same depth as previously, with the stem about 2in (5cm) away from the stake. Fill in the soil around the tree and firm in. Tie to the stake, and mulch with a layer of well-rotted manure.

Rootstocks: 'Quince A' half-standards are sometimes grafted to seedling pear rootstocks. Space trees 15ft (4.5m) apart.

Maintenance: Water if the weather is hot and dry. Feed and mulch occasionally. Thin fruit in early summer if a heavy crop has set.

Pruning and training: For the first few years, cut back the leaders of the main branches to two-thirds of the previous season's growth, to an outward-facing bud. Prune to three buds any badly-placed shoots crossing over the centre. If there is space within the framework, leave the other shoots to fill it so that it is well-shaped. Thereafter, prune lightly, pruning out dead, diseased and crossing wood.

Propagation: Usually by grafting on to quince, thorn or seedling pear rootstocks. They can also be grown from seed.

Harvesting and storing: Pick the fruits in late autumn and allow to decay or 'blet' for several weeks. Store in a cool place, not touching, on slatted trays. When the flesh is brown and soft, scoop it out with a spoon. Do not eat the seeds.

Average yields: 30lb (13.5kg) from a mature half-standard tree.

Pests and diseases: Few, apart from occasional attack by leaf-eating caterpillars.

Recommended varieties:

'Dutch' is a small, weeping tree that bears very large, russet brown fruits.

'Nottingham' (organic) is prolific, but of straggly habit and produces small, well-flavoured fruits.

'Royal' is a fairly upright tree that flowers in late spring and crops well.

'Senlac' (organic) has thorny wood, long, narrow, dark leaves and quite small fruit.

Companion plants: Tansy, chives.

ABOVE **Medlar 'Nottingham'**

NAME: MELON
CUCUMIS MELO
FAMILY: CUCURBITACEAE

Type: Tender annual

USDA zone: 9–10 outside, 8 under glass

Description: Cantaloupe melons have rough, grooved, greyish-green or buff skin, with green, orange or pink flesh. They grow well in a cold greenhouse or cold frame. Netted or musk melons are small, round or oval with yellowish-green or buff skin that has fine or coarse fibrous netting. Some varieties of melon need a heated greenhouse to succeed. Winter (*Casaba*) melons are large and oval with yellow or green, ribbed skin.

Where to grow: In cold areas a greenhouse will provide the warmth melons need. They can be planted in the borders or in growing bags.

When to plant: Sow seed in mid-spring and set the plants in their final growing positions from late spring.

How to grow: Sow seed singly in 3in (7.5cm) pots filled with compost. Cover the pots with glass and keep at a minimum temperature of 65°F (18°C). Harden off seedlings and plant out when they have three or four true leaves.

Cold frame: In mid spring, dig some well-rotted manure into the soil in the centre of the cold frame. Mound up the soil, and plant one hardened-off seedling into the mound, leaving 1in (2.5cm) of the ball of soil above the surface. Water in and close the cold frame.

Under glass: Plant the seedlings in the greenhouse borders, individually in 10in (25cm) pots, or two seedlings to a growing bag, leaving 1in (2.5cm) of the soil ball above the surface. Place a cane behind each plant. Install a support system before planting, stretching wires horizontally at 12in (30cm) intervals, 15in (37.5cm) from the glass to the ridge. Tie the supporting canes to them.

Maintenance:

Under glass: Pinch out the growing point of the plant when it reaches the ridge – the stem will be about 6ft (1.8m) high. Pinch out the growing tip of each lateral when five leaves have been produced. The male flowers appear first, then the female. When six female flowers are open, hand-pollinate by removing a male flower and pushing it gently into the centre of the female flower (these have a slight swelling just behind the petals). Pollination is best done at midday. When the melons are the size of marbles, thin the fruits and pinch out the stem two leaves beyond the fruit to stop the side shoots. Remove the fruit so that there is just one melon on each lateral. Remove any further shoots that appear. Water regularly and damp down. Start liquid feeding when the fruits are golf ball size, and continue every week until they begin to ripen. Use a special melon net to support each fruit once it reaches the size of a tennis ball, or tie net slings to the wires to support the fruits which can break under their own weight.

Cold frame: When the fifth true leaf appears, pinch out the growing point to encourage the development of side shoots. A few weeks later, take the four strongest shoots and train each to a corner of the cold frame. When the male and female flowers appear, open the cold frame during the day to allow insects to pollinate the flowers. In cold, wet weather, keep the frame closed and pollinate by hand. Thin the fruit and stop the shoots by pinching out the stem two leaves beyond the fruit and removing unwanted fruit so there is one melon per shoot. Pinch out the tip of each of the four main shoots. Place a tile under each fruit for support. Control ventilation carefully at all times. Water/feed as for greenhouse melons.

Pruning and training: No further pruning or training required.

Propagation: From seed.

Harvesting and storing: Pick when thoroughly ripe. Will keep for a few days in a refrigerator.

Average yields: 4–6 fruits per plant.

Pests and diseases: Slugs, cucumber mosaic virus, powdery mildew (outdoors), leaf scorch.

Recommended varieties:

Cantaloupe: 'Ogen' produces small fruits with yellow and green skins.

'Sweetheart' is one of the best varieties for growing in cool conditions.

'Minnesota Midget' is a small-fruited melon with fast ripening fruit.

Netted or Musk: 'Blenheim Orange' is a greenhouse variety with large, firm fruits, red-orange flesh, and a very good flavour.

'Tiger' has a yellow and green striped skin and is suitable for greenhouses and cold frames.

Companion plants: Sweet corn, sunflower, morning glory flowers.

ABOVE **Melon growing**

NAME: **MULBERRY**
MORUS NIGRA
FAMILY: **MORACEAE**

Type: Perennial

USDA zone: 5–8

Description: Black mulberry trees are attractive and ornamental, with decorative leaves and bark. The fruits resemble loganberries and are almost black when fully ripe, with a sharp, sweet flavour. Growth is very slow and the trees will not fruit for around seven years. They reach an eventual height of 20–30ft (6–9m) and are self-fertile. Mature tree branches become brittle and crooked with age.

Where to grow: Mulberries prefer a rich, fertile, well-drained, moisture-retentive soil (with a pH of 5.5–7). They enjoy a warm, sunny, sheltered position. Plant against a south-facing fence or wall in colder areas.

When to plant: Plant between late autumn and winter. In cold areas, plant in spring.

How to grow: Prepare a 3 x 3 ft (90 x 90cm) planting area for each tree before planting. Dig a hole deep and wide enough to take the roots when they are spread out. Before planting, either drive in a stake that will reach just below the lowest branches, or construct a wire support on a fence or wall, with the horizontal wires 9in (23cm) apart. Plant a 3–5 year-old tree to the same depth as the original soil level, carefully as the roots are very brittle. Refill the hole with soil and firm. Tie the tree to the stake with a tree tie, or tie the branches to the wall wires. Water in well and mulch with well-rotted manure.

Maintenance: Water in very dry weather. Apply a balanced fertilizer in late winter, and mulch with well-rotted manure in spring.

Pruning and training: For trees planted in open space, cut back any laterals longer than 12in (30cm) that are not needed for the framework to four or five buds. Do this during the first and second winters. Subsequently, cut out any dead, diseased, damaged or crossed branches. Cut mulberry branches 'bleed', so keep pruning to a minimum. For wall-trained trees, train in the main branches 15–18in (37.5–45cm) apart during the summer. Cut out the breastwood, and any branches that grow inwards towards the wall. At the end of the summer, tie down the leaders. When they are the desired length, cut them back to one bud on the previous year's growth in spring. Cut the side shoots to four or five leaves in mid/late summer.

Propagation: By air layering or by 7in (17.5cm) hardwood cuttings taken with a heel in mid-autumn.

Harvesting and storing: Pick the fruit in late summer when it is fully ripe and almost black. For cooking, it can be slightly under-ripe. Eat fresh or cooked, or freeze.

Average yields: Depend on the age of the tree and the winter weather.

Pests and diseases: Scale insects, dieback.

Recommended varieties:

'Chelsea', also known as 'King James', (organic) fruits early, bearing delicious, dark red fruit.

'Wellington' has an abundance of fine fruit.

Companion plants: Grape vines, lemon balm, chives, nasturtiums, marigolds.

NAME: **NECTARINE**
PRUNES PERSICA VAR. NECTARINA
FAMILY: **ROSACEAE**

Type: Evergreen
USDA zone: 8–10
Description: Nectarines have glossy leaves that secrete an aromatic oil. The small, white, star-shaped flowers are also scented. In temperate zones, trees need to be grown under glass for at least part of the year. They are self-fertile.

Where to grow: Nectarines need a fertile, moisture-retentive, free-draining, slightly acid soil (pH6–6.5), and a sunny, sheltered site. A south-west, south, or south-east wall is ideal for a fan. They can be grown under glass.

When to plant: Plant bare-rooted plants in late autumn, container-grown ones in early autumn.

How to grow:

Bush trees: Plant bare-rooted trees in prepared ground. Dig a hole wide and deep enough to accommodate the spread roots. Planting distances vary according to the tree's vigour.

Fans: Plant 12ft (3.6m) apart, about 9in (23cm) from the wall. Angle the stem slightly in to the wall. Buy a 2–3 year-old tree with eight or more branches to get it off to a good start. Usually grown on 'St Julien A' rootstock.

Maintenance: Water regularly in dry weather; never allow the soil around the roots to dry out. Place netting or a piece of hessian over the trees in early spring to protect them from frost damage. Remove the netting during the day to allow insects to pollinate the flowers. The blossoms open very early, when insects are scarce, however, so hand-pollination may be necessary. Protect the trees from bird damage at fruit time and again in winter. Apply a high potash liquid feed every two weeks from late spring to late summer. If the crop is heavy, thin to one fruit every 6–9in (15–23cm).

Under glass: Ventilate the closed greenhouse when the temperature reaches 60–65°F (16–18°C). Spray the floor in hot weather and

ABOVE **Ripe, juicy nectarines**

water the plants regularly. Use a high potash liquid feed from the start of flowering until the fruit is almost mature. Hand-pollinate. Keep the greenhouse cool after harvesting the fruit.

Pruning and training:

Two-year-old bush trees: Prune in early spring. Cut back strong branches to half their length and weaker branches to a third of their length. There should be 3–5 strong branches, as horizontal as possible. Remove all blossom produced in the season after planting.

Three-year-old bush tree: In spring, cut back the new growth by one half and any new growth necessary to open up the tree to keep a well-shaped framework.

Established bush trees: Remove any diseased, broken or dead branches in spring. After the annual harvest remove some unproductive branches to encourage new growth – fruit will only develop on young shoots.

Fans: In late winter, shorten by a third the leaders of 2–3 year old trees, cutting to a downward pointing bud. In summer, let the leading shoots on each rib grow and train three shoots on each branch outwards. Tie them to canes and let shoots grow at 4in (10cm) intervals. In late summer, pinch out the growing point of each lateral and tie the laterals (which will fruit the following summer) to canes on the wires. Thereafter, every year in late spring, remove any shoots growing towards or away from the wall. Leave any shoots with flower buds at their base with one or two leaves. Select a replacement lateral at the base of each leader, and a reserve in the middle. Allow a lateral to extend the fruit-carrying lateral. When the extension has six leaves and both the base and middle or reserve laterals are 18in (45cm) long, pinch out the growing points. Cut the fruited laterals back to their replacements after harvest.

Propagation: Usually by chip- or T-budding in summer.

Harvesting and storing: Harvest the fruits when fully ripe and eat as soon as possible. Store unwrapped in a box lined with tissue in a cool place for a few days.

Average yields:

Bush: 30–60lb (13.5–27kg) per mature tree.
Fan: 10lb–12lb (4.5–5.4 kg) per mature tree.

Pests and diseases: Red spider mite under glass, also aphids and mildew.

Recommended varieties:

'Early Rivers' (organic) has large, yellow fruits, flushed red, with sweet juicy flesh and an excellent flavour.

'Lord Napier' is a heavy cropper, with large, yellow-orange fruits that have a crimson flush.

'Humboldt' has medium to large, yellow-orange fruit with a deep crimson flush and is good in greenhouses. The fruit ripens in late summer.

Companion plants: Garlic, chives, nettles.

NAME: OLIVE
OLEA EUROPAEA
FAMILY: OLEACEAE

Type: Evergreen
USDA zone: 9–10
Description: Olive trees are gnarled and twisted with long, thin, dark leaves, the undersides of which are silver. The grape-sized fruit have edible seeds with a rich, oily taste. Most cultivars are self-fertile, but they are also pollinated by insects and wind. Cross-pollination increases yields.

Where to grow: Olives grow in a wide variety of soils, but prefer those with low to medium fertility. They grow well on alkaline soils. They prefer full sun and a well-drained site. Shelter from the wind in exposed areas. They can be planted in containers, but are unlikely to fruit. They can also be grown under glass, but in conditions that are not too hot or humid.

When to plant: Plant bare-rooted trees when dormant in autumn or spring. Set out container-grown plants any time if the weather is suitable.

How to grow: Olives grow well in subtropical areas with a temperature range of 41–77°F (5–25°C). In temperate regions they seldom flower or fruit, but are sometimes grown as

RIGHT **Ripe black olives ready for picking**

ornamentals. Plant from 22ft (7m) to 40ft (12m) apart each way, and stake to prevent wind damage. Trees grown in the open will flower and fruit 3–4 years after planting.

Maintenance: When the trees are in active growth, apply an annual top dressing of an organic fertilizer with medium nitrogen levels. Water regularly in dry weather and mulch with organic matter. Keep free from weeds. Thin the fruit by hand where they are close together on the stem, or remove excess fruits individually.

Pruning and training: Cut back any dead, diseased or crossing branches. Only light pruning will be necessary because olives bear fruit on the previous season's growth.

Propagation: From seed, but the plants may not come true. Take cuttings with a heel in late summer or hardwood cuttings 12in (30cm) long during winter.

Harvesting and storing: Green olives are picked unripe and are usually pickled. Black olives are picked when ripe and pressed for oil. Gather black olives to eat when they are black and firm, pack in dry salt to dehydrate them, then store in oil.

Average yields: In Mediterranean areas, olive trees fruit at around eight years-old and produce around 60lb (27kg) of olives per tree.

Pests and diseases: Scale insects, root-knot nematodes. Verticillium wilt can affect trees in the open. Trees under cover can be troubled by whitefly, thrips and red spider mite.

Recommended varieties:
Usually only unnamed species available. Subtropical cultivars include 'Allegra' and 'Oblonga'. Of the green pickling varieties, 'Queen Manzanilla' cultivars are the largest.

Companion plants: None known.

NAME: **ORANGE**
CITRUS SINENSIS
FAMILY: **RUTACEAE**

Type: Tender evergreen

USDA zone: 9–11

Description: The orange tree has beautiful, deep green, aromatic foliage. It is self-fertile and many varieties produce seedless fruits. Bitter Seville oranges are grown for making marmalade and preserves.

Where to grow: Oranges like a light, sandy, slightly acid (pH6–6.5) well-drained soil. They like a sunny, sheltered position. In temperate regions, they do best under glass, but can be placed outdoors in summer. If grown in large containers, they can be moved indoors before the first frosts. Or grow in a conservatory.

When to plant: Plant young trees in small pots and pot on to larger containers. Pot on during winter. Container-grown trees can be planted outside during spring or autumn.

How to grow: Outside planting distances will vary according to the vigour of the cultivar. To obtain the most light, plant the trees 25ft (7.5m) apart. In warm countries, plant them 15–20ft (4.5–6m) apart each way.

RIGHT **Calamondin orange**

Maintenance: Water regularly. Apply a blood, fish and bone meal dressing in early spring and summer, and water in well. Spray with liquid organic feed throughout the year. In winter, feed should contain trace elements like iron and zinc to prevent yellowing foliage and stunted growth.

Pruning and training: Shorten the main branches of newly-planted trees by a third in the first year to encourage lateral growth. Prune out dead, diseased or crossing branches after harvesting. Trim new growth in early spring if necessary to keep a good shape.

Propagation: T-budding is the usual method. Cuttings can also be taken, or the fruit can be raised from seed. Seedlings are slow to bear fruit and do not always come true.

Harvesting and storing: The trees crop when they are seven to eight years old. The fruit does not all ripen at once, and harvesting can continue over many weeks. Pick when well coloured, or leave on the tree for up to six months until required. Stored in layers of dry sand in a wooden box in a cool place, the fruit should keep for a couple of months.

Average yield: A well-grown, ten-year-old tree can produce about 500 fruits in winter.

Pests and diseases: Under glass, oranges can be attacked by all kinds of insects, but grown outside are relatively trouble free. Soft soap sprays can be useful for dealing with insects. Look out for red spider mite, aphids, scale and mealy bugs and sooty mould.

Recommended varieties:

'Navelina' is a distinctive navel orange that was introduced to America during the 19th century. 'Jaffa' is a large, thick-skinned seedless variety. 'Maltese' is a blood orange, with sweet flesh tinged with red.

Companion plants: In warm countries, oak and guava are often grown near orange trees.

NAME: PAPAYA
CARICA PAPAYA
FAMILY: ANNONACEAE

Type: Perennial

USDA zone: 4–8

Description: Papaya, or paw-paw, is a slender, tropical tree that grows to 12–15ft (3.6–4.5m). The ripe fruit has greenish yellow skin, speckled with brown, and orange, custardy flesh. Plants are male, female, and hermaphrodite.

Where to grow: Papayas enjoy a well-drained, fertile soil (pH6–7) and full sunlight. Protect from strong winds. They look attractive in containers, but will not fruit well. They can be grown under glass.

When to plant: Plant young trees in spring.

How to grow: Plant trees 10ft (3m) apart and stake while young. Male and female flowers are produced on separate plants and one male tree can pollinate five or six female ones. The flowers are also pollinated by insects and wind. Sow seed in trays, and transplant the seedlings when large enough to handle. Harden off and plant out when they are 12–18in (30–45cm) tall in groups of three or four, thinning to one female plant after flowering starts.

Under glass: Transplant the seedlings when they are 8–10in (20–25cm) tall into prepared greenhouse beds or 14in (35cm) pots. Maintain a temperature of 72°F (22°C) and above, and and humidity of 60–70 per cent. Apply a liquid feed every month, and water regularly.

Maintenance: Apply a balanced organic fertilizer to outdoor plants every four months during the growing season. Water regularly in dry weather and mulch to conserve moisture.

Pruning and training: Very little pruning is necessary, apart from removing unproductive lateral branches. Prune to 12in (30cm) from the

133

ground after fruiting. Select the strongest new shoot as the leader and prune back the others.

Propagation: From seed or by grafting.

Harvesting and storing: Ripe papayas are slightly soft with black specks on their skin. Leave to ripen on the trees before picking, or harvest slightly under-ripe and store for up to 14 days at 50–55°F (10–13°C) and 70 per cent humidity.

Average yields: 30–40 fruits per tree.

Pests and diseases: (outdoors) Root knot nematodes, anthracnose, bunchy top virus; (under glass) aphids, thrips, whitefly, mealybugs.

Recommended varieties:

'Solo' is of uniform fruit shape and size with high productivity and excellent quality.

'Waimanalo' is an excellent variety with yellow-orange flesh.

'Sunrise' has reddish-orange flesh.

Companion plants: None known.

NAME: **PASSION FRUIT**
PASSIFLORA EDULIS
FAMILY: **PASSIFLORACEAE**

Type: Evergreen

USDA zone: 9–10

Description: Passion fruits are tropical and subtropical vines grown in places including Hawaii, Australia, Africa and New Zealand. The fruits are about the same size as a plum, but with leathery, wrinkled, purple skin, yellowish-orange flesh and crunchy seeds. They have a distinctive smell and taste.

Where to grow: In a humus-rich, moist, well-drained soil in greenhouse borders or in pots. Passion fruit is happier under glass, but potted plants can be set outside in summer when the temperature is at least 60°F (16°C).

When to plant: Plant seedlings in their growing positions in spring or early summer. Re-pot container-grown plants annually in early spring.

How to grow: Sow fresh seed on the surface of a tray filled with moist peat-based compost. Space half an inch (12mm) apart evenly over the compost. Spread a thin layer of compost over the seed, almost burying them. Maintain a temperature of around 75°F (24°C), ensuring the seeds have plenty of light to aid germination. This can be erratic, anything from two–eight weeks. Pot the seedlings up in compost-filled 3in (7.5cm) pots. Pot on into their final container when they are between 12–18in (30–45cm) high. When planting greenhouse borders, plant two seedlings 24in (60cm) apart and pinch out the growing tip. Support using wires running horizontally along the side of the greenhouse, 9in (23cm) apart, and finishing 18in (45cm) below the ridge. Keep the wires 12–15in (30–37.5cm) away from the glass to prevent the plants from scorching.

LEFT **Papaya fruit and tropical flowers**

Maintenance: The plants need plenty of water because they have such an abundance of leaves. Water daily in hot weather, but just once a week in winter to keep the roots moist. During summer, hang plastic netting 6in (15cm) below the greenhouse roof glass and train two leaders on to the supports. Pot-grown fruit will need the same support. Hand-pollinate using a soft brush, then liquid feed every two weeks until the fruits ripen. Give container-grown plants an annual top dressing of fresh compost.

Pruning and training: In winter, cut back the current season's fruit bearing growth close to the framework stems. Never hard prune as this will promote vigorous growth and few fruits. In spring, train two new leaders on to the supports, training in any new growth too. Remove the tips of single-stemmed plants.

Propagation: Take cuttings in late spring from new 7–8in (17.5–20cm) shoots, with a 'heel'. Pot up several into 3.5in (8cm) pots filled with sandy compost and place in a propagator, or place the pots in clear plastic bags and keep at a temperature of 75°F (24°C). Pot the rooted seedlings up individually. Pot on again when they are 12in (30cm) high.

Harvesting and storing: Pick the fruits when fully ripe as they will not ripen further once they have been removed from the vine. They should come off at a touch, but a net can be placed underneath the vines and the fruits allowed to fall off into the net. Eat them as soon as possible.

Average yields: 7.5–15lb (3.57kg) per plant.

Pests and diseases: Red spider mite, whitefly, aphids.

Recommended varieties:

Purple form: 'Purple Giant' is a large variety of passion fruit that is dark purple when mature.

'Kahuna' has very large, medium purple fruits with a delicious flavour.

'Frederick' originated in California and has large, nearly oval fruits with a slightly tart flavour.

Yellow form: 'Golden Giant' with its large, yellow fruits, originated in Australia.

'Brazilian Golden' has extra-large, scented flowers and large, golden-yellow fruits.

Companion plants: Plant pot marigolds and tobacco plants in the greenhouse.

RIGHT **Passion flower**

NAME: **PEACH**
PRUNUS PERSICA
FAMILY: **ROSACEAE**

Type: Perennial

USDA zone: 9–10

Description: Peach trees are self-fertile and have long, tapering, light green leaves and bear attractive, single, pink flowers in early spring. The fruits have a downy skin.

Where to grow: Peach trees enjoy a deep, fertile, slightly acid soil (pH6.5–7). Maximum sun and a sheltered, frost-free site with good drainage are essential, but the soil should be moisture-retentive. A south-facing wall is ideal. Grow in a greenhouse in cooler climates.

When to plant: During the dormant season from late autumn to early spring. Mid-winter is ideal because growth starts very early.

ABOVE **'Crimson Lady'** peaches growing.

How to grow outside: Before planting, fork in some organic fertilizer. Dig a hole deep and wide enough to take the fully-extended roots. Plant to the depth of the soil mark on the stem, then apply a 2–3in (5–7.5cm) mulch of well-rotted manure. Fans will need a support system. Choose a 4ft (1.2m) length of wall or fence and secure wires to it with vine eyes. Space wires 6in (15cm) apart leaving at least 6–9in (15–23cm) between the wall and the wires. Plant stems inclining slightly towards the wall.

Planting distances:

Bushes: Plant 'St Julien A' rootstock 15–18ft (4.5–5.4m) apart; 'Brompton' or seedling peach rootstock 18–24ft (5.4–7.4m) apart.

Fans: Use 'St Julien A' rootstock and plant 11–15ft (3.5–4.5m) apart.

Under glass: Use 'St Julien A' rootstock and plant 11–15ft (3.5–4.5m) apart against wires.

Maintenance:

Outside: In early spring apply blood, fish and bonemeal (two handfuls per sq yd/sq m) around the plants. Mulch annually with well-rotted manure. Protect blossom with horticultural fleece when frost is forecast. When the fruitlets are about the size of a hazelnut, thin to one per cluster. When they reach the size of a walnut, leave one fruit every 6–9in (15–23cm). Water regularly in dry areas. Improve poor pollination by hand-pollinating.

Under glass: Keep the greenhouse as cold as possible during winter so the tree remains dormant. In spring and summer, let the temperature reach 50°F (10°C) before ventilating. Spray daily except at flowering time. Flowers bloom early, so may have to be hand-pollinated. Feed weekly with an organic liquid fertilizer during the growing season.

Pruning and training:

Bushes: Prune a feathered maiden planted in late autumn/winter in early spring. Choose three or four well-spaced laterals with the top one about 3ft (90cm) from the ground. Prune back the leader just above the top lateral, and prune to two-thirds each of the chosen laterals. Remove all unwanted ones. In summer, remove any badly-placed shoots. The following spring, choose laterals and sub-laterals to form the basic framework and cut them back by one half to a bud. Prune the other sub-laterals to about 4–5in (10–12.5cm). When the tree is established, keep the centre open by removing some of the older fruited shoots every summer. Cut out unproductive branches occasionally.

Fans: For first-year plants, select two laterals to form the main arms, one either side of the maiden tree stem and 12in (30cm) from the ground. Cut out the leader just above the higher lateral. Cut back each arm to about 15in (37.5cm), to a strong bud, to encourage side shoots or 'ribs' to develop. Cut back the other lower laterals to one bud. Attach canes to the wires at an angle of 40° and tie each main arm to a cane. In summer, select two side shoots on top of each arm and one underneath. Tie to canes evenly spaced and attached to the wires. Pinch back the other shoots to one leaf. For second and third year plants, shorten each side shoot or rib by a third in late winter, pruning back to a bud. As more ribs develop, tie them evenly on to the wires.

Established fans: Remove the shoots growing inwards towards the wall or outwards from it in spring. Pinch out the growth buds on the flowering laterals, leaving one at the base, one in the middle, and one at the top. Cut back each shoot to six leaves in late spring. After harvesting, cut out the fruited lateral and tie in its replacement.

Propagation: Usually by budding or grafting.

Harvesting and storing: Pick the fruit as it ripens, when the flesh around the stalk is soft. Handle carefully. Store unwrapped in a tissue-lined box for about a week, or dry, bottle or freeze (remove stones before freezing).

Average yields: 30–60lb (13.6–27kg) per bush; 12–25lb (5.4–11.3kg) per fan.

Pests and diseases: Birds, aphids, earwigs, red spider mite, peach leaf curl, canker, powdery mildew.

Recommended varieties:
'Red Haven' crops well and has firm, juicy, yellow flesh.
'Peregrine' is a reliable, high-yielding variety, good for growing against an outdoor wall.
'Hayles Early' is an early cropper and a good choice for growing outdoors.
'Humboldt' is a heavy cropper with golden flesh and a rich flavour, that is ideal for greenhouse cultivation.

Companion plants: Garlic, tansy, chives, nettles.

NAME: PEANUT
ARACHIS HYPOGAEA
FAMILY: LEGUMINOSAE

Type: Tender annual

USDA zone: 7 and warmer

Description: Peanuts are produced from the fertilized, yellow flowers of a tropical, peanut-like plant. After pollination, the stalks lengthen and penetrate the soil where the immature fruits develop into peanuts. They are self-pollinating members of the legume family, and there are four main varieties under cultivation around the world: Spanish, Valencia, Virginia and Runner. Spanish has two seeds per pod, Valencia has up to four seeds per pod, and Virginia and Runner have two large seeds per pod.

Where to grow: Peanuts thrive in a calcium-rich, loose, well-drained soil (pH5.5–6.5). They need a sunny, sheltered site; too much shade may result in lower yields and slower growth. They can also be grown under glass in greenhouse beds, large pots or growing bags.

When to plant: Mid/late spring is ideal. To grow well, plants need an average temperature of 68–86°F (20–30°C). In temperate climates, sow under glass.

How to grow:

Outside: Plant the seeds 2–3 (5–7.5cm) deep. Sow five seeds per 1ft (30cm) row, 3in (7.5cm) apart. Protect with cloches.

Under glass: Plant seeds in trays or small pots at a temperature above 68°F (20°C). When the seedlings are 4–6in (10–15cm) high, transplant into the greenhouse border, large pots or growing bags. Maintain a temperature of 68°F (20°C), and reduce humidity at flowering time.

Maintenance: Hand weed and water in dry weather. Do not water during the flowering period as it can lead to poor pollination. Earth up around the roots when the plants are 6in (15cm) high. Peanuts flower above ground, but the pods develop below the soil. The flowers begin to bloom 30 to 40 days after emergence. After pollination, the stalk or peg below the fertilized ovary curves downwards, and takes around 10 days to penetrate the soil.

Pruning and training: None necessary.

Propagation: From seed.

Harvesting and storing: 120–140 frost-free days are required for a good crop. Pods do not all mature at once. Harvest when the foliage begins to turn yellow in late summer to early autumn, checking whether they are ready by uprooting one or two pods. Dig up with a fork, shaking off any loose soil. Dry the pods by hanging the plants in a warm shed or garage. After one–two weeks, pull the pods from the plants and continue to dry. When dry, store in cool, dry, well-ventilated conditions. They will keep for several months.

Average yields: Single row 3310lb (1504.5kg) per acre (0.4047Ha), twin row 6140lb (2790kg) per acre (0.4047Ha).

Pests and diseases: Aphids, caterpillars and thrips outside, red spider mite, whitefly, fungal leaf spot, root and stem rot under glass. Rosette virus can also cause problems.

Recommended varieties:

Spanish: 'Pronto' and 'Spanco' are small-seeded, early maturing varieties, that usually produce pods near the tap roots.

'Valencia' is best for garden cultivation.

'New Mexico A', 'New Mexico C' and 'Georgia Red' have three or four seeds per pod. They mature early and are easy to harvest.

Virginia: 'NC7', 'NC9', and 'NC-Vll' all have large-seeds and a good flavour, but take longer to mature. They are popular for boiling or roasting.

Runner: 'Georgia Runner', 'Andru 93' and 'Georgia Green' produce high yields and are popular for commercial planting.

Companion plants: Corn, squash, coconuts.

LEFT **Newly emerged peanut seedling**
INSET **Harvested peanuts**

NAME: **PEAR**
PYRUS COMMUNIS VAR SATIVA
FAMILY: **ROSACEAE**

Type: Perennial

USDA zone: 6–8

Description: Pear trees have shiny leaves and delicious, apple-like fruit, elongated at the stalk end. They are as decorative as they are useful.

Where to grow: Pears need a deep, well-drained, moisture retentive, slightly acid soil (pH6.5–7). Standards and half-standards may be too big for the average garden, but pear trees can be grown as cordons, espaliers, fans, dwarf pyramids and bushes. They like a warm, sunny, sheltered site and grow well on east- and west-facing walls. Bush types can be cultivated as lawn specimens.

When to plant: Plant bare-rooted trees during the dormant period from autumn until spring. Set out container-grown plants at any time, if the weather is suitable.

How to grow: Plant two compatible cultivars for cross-pollination as pears are not fully self-fertile. Buy bushes as two-year-old trees if possible, and types that need supporting (such as cordons) as three-year-olds. Rootstocks sold by nurseries are often 'Quince A', so check before buying.Dig the soil well over an area of about 3ft (90cm) for each tree in early autumn. Remove perennial weeds and fork in some organic fertilizer. Plant the tree to the depth of its original soil level in a hole wide and deep enough for the extended roots. The rootstock union should be about 4in (10cm) above soil level. Stake bushes, spindlebushes, half-standards and standards. Support restricted forms such as fans from wires on a fence, wall or between posts.

Planting distances:

Bush: Rootstock 'Quince C' 11ft (3.5m) between each tree; 18ft (5.4m) between each row. Rootstock 'Quince A' 15ft (4.5m) between each tree; 15ft (4.5m) between each row.

Cordon: Rootstock 'Quince A' or 'Quince C' 30in (75cm) between each tree; 6ft (1.8m) between each row.

Espalier: Rootstock 'Quince C' 11ft (3.5m) between each tree; 6ft (1.8m) between each row. Rootstock 'Quince A' 11ft (3.5m) between each tree; 6ft (1.8m) between each row.

Fan: 11ft (3.5m) between each tree for rootstock 'Quince C', 14ft (4.2m) between each tree for rootstock 'Quince A' .

Dwarf pyramid: 4ft (1.2m) between each tree and 6ft (1.8m) between each row for rootstock 'Quince C', 8ft (2.4m) between each tree and 6ft (1.8m) between each row for rootstock 'Quince A'.

ABOVE **Pears growing on a tree**

Maintenance: Keep weed free and water regularly in dry weather. Mulch newly-planted young trees with well-rotted manure or compost, keeping it away from the stems. The fruit will benefit if nitrogen fertilizer is added. Thin after the drop in early summer, when the fruitlets turn down, to two fruits per cluster. Support heavy crops by 'maypoling'– see page 55.

Pruning and training:

Two-year-old spindlebush: In winter of the second year onwards, remove any upright laterals and prune the remainder by a quarter, to a bud. Cut back the central leader to two-thirds of the previous season's growth. to an opposite facing bud. Thereafter, in mid summer, tie down new laterals. Cut back the leader to a weaker lateral and tie up as the new leader.

Three-year-old cordon: From the third year onwards, if the previously-pruned shoots have grown, cut them back just before the leaves fall to the mature wood. In late spring, when the leader has passed the top wire, cut back extension growth to its starting point. In mid-summer, cut back the leader. Prune the side shoots, and prune to three leaves any mature laterals longer than 9in (23cm) that are growing away from the main stem.

Spurs: If spur systems become overcrowded as the tree matures, thin to two–three fruit buds.

Three-year-old espaliers: From mid-summer to early autumn, train the second tier of branches by training the shoot from the top bud vertically up the cane. Train the shoots from the two lower buds at an angle of 45° to the main stem, and tie them to canes fastened on to the wires. Cut back competing growths from the main stem to three leaves. Prune laterals from the horizontal arms to three leaves above the basal cluster.

Mature espaliers: In late spring, when the final tier is reached, cut back the new terminal growths of the vertical and horizontal arms to their starting point. Thereafter, prune the espaliers every summer as for cordons.

Three-year-old dwarf pyramids: In late autumn to late winter, cut the central leader to leave 9in (23cm) of new growth. Cut to a bud on the opposite side of the previous pruning. From mid to late summer, prune the leaders of the side branches to six leaves. Cut back the laterals to three leaves and sub-laterals to one leaf beyond the basal cluster. From late autumn to late winter, prune the central leader to leave 9in (23cm) of new growth. Shorten the branches to downward-pointing buds to maintain the horizontal set of the fruiting arms. Thereafter, in late spring, cut back the leader when the tree has reached its required height, thin fruiting

LEFT **Pear blossom 'Conference'**

spurs, and maintain the pyramid shape by removing vigorous shoots. The mature tree should be about 7ft (2.1m) high.

Propagation: By whip-and-tongue grafting or chip- or T-budding on to 'Quince A' or 'Quince C' rootstocks.

Harvesting and storing: Pick early-ripening varieties when the fruits are full-sized, but before the fully-ripe stage. Cut the stalks and then leave the pears for a few days to develop their full flavour. Eat them as they ripen because they do not store well. Harvest later varieties when they part easily from the tree and will ripen in storage. Store, unwrapped, on slatted trays in a cool place. They are ready to eat when the fruit begins to soften near the stalk.

Average yields per mature tree or bush:
Standard 100–250lb (45.5–113.5kg)
Half-standard 50–125lb (23–57kg)
Bush 40–100lb (18–45.5kg)
Spindlebush 30–160lb (13.6–72.5kg)
Dwarf bush 40–60lb (18–27.2kg)
Dwarf pyramid 8–12lb (3.5–5.4kg)
Fan 12–24lb (5.4–11kg)
Espalier 15–25lb (7–11.3kg)
Cordon 4–6lb (1.8–2.7kg)

Pests and diseases: Birds, rabbits, wasps, aphids, winter moth caterpillars, pear leaf blister mites, scab, brown rot, fireblight.

Recommended varieties:
'Conference' (organic) is an old variety that has long, narrow fruits with firm, juicy flesh. It crops well without any need for a pollinator.
'Doyenne du Comice' (organic) has outstanding texture and flavour. It needs a warm site.
'Durondeau' (organic) is a compact pear that crops heavily. Its leaves turn fiery red in autumn.

Companion plants: Tansy, chives, spinach, borage, nasturtiums.

NAME: PECAN NUTS
CARYA ILLINOENSIS
FAMILY: JUGLANDACEAE

Type: Perennial
USDA zone: 6–9

Description: The pecan is the Texas state tree and can grow to 180ft (54m) high. The bark is rough, scaly and pale grey or whitish brown, and the leaves are a dark yellow-green, smooth to slightly hairy on top. The nuts, which are long and pointed with a thin shell, grow in clusters of 3–11 with husks that split into four sections.

Where to grow: The tree enjoys a deep, fertile, well-drained soil (pH6–6.5) and full sun. Pecans have massive root systems and should be planted at least 35ft (10.5m) apart.

When to plant: Plant bare-rooted trees from early winter to early spring. Plant container grown trees any time if the weather is suitable.

How to grow: Trim off all broken roots before planting. Dig a hole big that is big enough to accommodate the extended root system. Backfill with soil to allow the tree to settle. Root damage can be caused by planting too deep, so plant the tree to the depth it was in the nursery. Cut back bare-rooted trees by half and water thoroughly. Pecans are wind pollinated and male and female flowers do not open at the same time, so plant them within 35ft (10.5m) of another variety, or a native tree.

Maintenance: Keep young trees free from weeds. Keep the soil well watered and mulched to ensure rapid growth and good quality nut production. Apply frequent, small amounts of a nitrogenous fertilizer during the first few years. Apply zinc sprays between early and mid spring for rapid growth.

Pruning and training: Pecans naturally take on a central-leader shape. Young trees often have 2–5 leaders growing from one point on the trunk. Remove all but one vertical trunk. Cut the central leader back to half in late winter/early spring. Several shoots will then develop just below the cut. For the first few years, during spring, leave the strongest of these shoots and remove the other shoots to within 6–8in (15–20cm) of the cut back. Permanent branches develop 6ft (1.8m) above the ground. Keep the lower trunk side shoots short by pinching out the growing points as necessary. If the tree has too many branches, thin them out as necessary. Mature trees need little pruning. Remove dead wood and low-hanging branches during late winter.

Propagation: Pecans do not come true from seed. Propagate by whip-and-tongue grafting on to vigorous pecan seedling rootstocks.

Harvesting and storing: Grafted trees will begin bearing nuts in 4–7 years. The nuts are mature when the hull splits four ways exposing the kernel. Harvest from mid to late autumn by shaking or thrashing the branches and collecting the fallen nuts. Remove the husks and dry the nuts for several weeks. Store in a cool place.

Average yields: 40–60 nuts per lb (450g), depending on growing conditions and variety.

Pests and diseases: Aphids, nematodes, pecan scab, powdery mildew, *Phytophthora* root rots, pecan weevil.

Recommended varieties:

Early pollen-shedding: 'Caddo' is scab resistant with attractive foliage and ripens early.

'Cape Fear' is scab resistant and bears fruit in 5–7 years.

'Cheyenne' is susceptible to aphids but is a very productive, smaller tree with high-quality nuts.

Late pollen-shedding: 'Sioux' is easy to train and produces small, high-quality nuts.

'Choctaw' has beautiful foliage, resists scab, and has high yields of large, good-quality nuts.

'Mohawk' is an early maturing variety with beautiful foliage and heavy yields.

Companion plants: Pot marigolds, petunias, nasturtiums, garlic.

ABOVE **Pecans growing on the tree**

NAME: **PINEAPPLE**
ANANAS COMOSUS
FAMILY: **BROMELIACEAE**

Type: Short-lived perennial

USDA zone: 10–11

Description: The pineapple is an exotic tropical fruit. Its rosette top radiates dagger-like leaves produced during the first year. In the second year, a flowering stalk arises from the centre of the plant. It produces light blue flowers that open row by row over a period of about two weeks, starting at the bottom of the plant. When the petals of the last flower have dried, the fruit, which has succulent, juicy, sweet, yellow flesh begins to develop.

Where to grow: Pineapples enjoy a sandy, medium loam soil (pH5–6.5) and need a sunny site, sheltered from the winds. They can be grown in pots under glass.

When to plant: Spring or autumn, but pineapples planted in spring will fruit earlier than those planted in autumn.

How to grow under glass: Prepare greenhouse borders incorporating plenty of organic matter and making sure that the drainage is good. The plants need a temperature of 64–80°F (18–27°C) with a humidity level of 70–80 per cent. Plant rooted cuttings or 'slips' in the greenhouse borders or in 12in (30cm) diameter pots filled with compost. Apply an organic liquid feed every three weeks or so. Maintain both temperature and humidity by spraying the plants and damping down the floor as necessary.

Maintenance: Feed the plants every two or three months with a medium potassium/high nitrogen fertilizer. Water regularly and apply an organic mulch to conserve moisture. At flowering time, place a support stake in the borders or pots to stop the young fruit being knocked over.

Pruning and training: None needed.

Propagation: Normally from the suckers that arise from the leaf axils, the base of the stem, or below the fruit. Cut them off with a sharp knife, dip them in a fungicide, and allow them to dry for three or four days. Remove the lower leaves and place them in pots of sandy compost. When they have rooted, pot them on. The terminal crown shoot can be used as a cutting to propagate the fruit. Cut through the top with a knife, taking care not to cut through the base of the shoot, with about half an inch (12mm) of the fruit attached to it. Dip the base into an organic

ABOVE **Pineapple plant**

fungicide and leave for two or three days to dry. Place in a pot of cutting compost and keep it at a temperature of 66–70°F (18–21°C). It should have rooted and be ready to pot on within a few weeks.

Harvesting and storing: Harvest the fruits when they begin to turn yellow and have a pleasant aroma. Cut the stem 1–2in (2.5–5cm) below each fruit. Store for a few weeks at a temperature of 46°F (8°C) and a humidity level of 90 per cent. The fruit can also be frozen.

Average yields: Cultivated pineapples yield two crops. The first 'ratoon' is a terminal large fruit. This is carefully removed and several new pineapples develop on the stalk inflorescence. The smaller fruits are harvested later.

Pests and diseases: Mealybugs, scale, mites, heart rot.

Recommended varieties:

'Red Spanish' has purple-hued skin, bright yellow flesh and spiny leaves. It is a little hardier than the others.

'Smooth Cayenne' does not have spines on the leaves. It makes a good container plant.

'Natal Queen' has spiny leaves. The fruits weigh 2–3lb (900g–1.35kg) each.

'Sugar Loaf' is a large, heavy variety with mildly sweet flesh.

Companion plants: None known.

NAME: **PLUM** *PRUNUS DOMESTICA* FAMILY: **ROSACEAE**

Type: Hardy perennial

USDA zone: 6–8

Description: Plums come in many varieties and a wide range of cultivars adapted to different climates. The trees flower early in the growing season, followed by succulent, ovoid fruits, sometimes sour, ranging in colour from dark purple through deep red to pale yellow. Many are self-fertile. The most widely used rootstock is 'St Julien A'.

Where to grow: Plums need a sheltered, frost-free site and prefer a deep, moisture-retentive well drained soil (pH6.5–7). Though culinary plums will tolerate some shade, generally they like lots of sun and low rainfall. A sunny, sheltered wall is ideal for fan-trained forms. They also make good lawn specimens.

When to plant: Late autumn is the best time.

How to grow: Plums can be grown as fans, cordons, espaliers, dwarf pyramids and bushes in the same way as apples. Prepare the ground thoroughly in early autumn. At planting time, dig a hole wide and deep enough for the fully-extended roots, and drive in a stake before planting. Stake for the first 5–6 years. For fan-trained trees, construct a support system with wires 6in (15cm) apart. Plant to the same depth as in the nursery, return the soil and firm in well. Tie the tree to the stake, or tie the branches of the fan to the support wires. Water in well.

Planting distances:

Standard: 20–25ft (6–7.5m) between each tree; 20–25ft (6–7.5m) between rows.

Half-standard: 18–20ft (5.4–6m) between each tree; 18–20ft (5.4–6m) between rows.

Fan: 12–15ft (3.6–4.5m) between each tree.

Bush: 14ft (4.2m) between each tree; 14ft (4.2m) between each row.

Pyramid: 10–12ft (3–3.6m) between each tree; 10–12ft (3–3.6m) between each row.

Maintenance: Hoe lightly to remove weeds from the base of the tree. Water regularly in dry weather. In spring, apply a nitrogen-rich liquid fertilizer. Cover trees with netting in spring and summer to prevent birds damaging flowers and fruit. If necessary, thin the fruitlets with scissors in early summer to 3–4in (7.5–10cm) apart.

Pruning and training: Do not prune plums in winter because of the risk of silver leaf disease.

Bush, standards, half-standards: In early spring of the first year, cut back the central stem of the maiden tree to a bud to 3ft (90cm) for a bush, 4.5ft (1.4m) for a half-standard, and 6ft (1.8m) for a standard. Shorten laterals to 3in (7.5cm). In late summer keep four evenly-spaced primary branches round the top of the stem. Pinch out the growing point of the others at 4–5 leaves. In the second years select four wide-angled branches: In late winter to early spring. Prune each leader back by half to outward-facing buds. Remove the remainder. Remove suckers and shoots on the main stem below the head in summer. In the third year, repeat the processes, but allow more secondary branches to develop so that there are about seven or eight outward-growing branches. Cut these back by two-thirds of the maiden growth to outward facing buds. Cut back unpruned laterals on the inside of the tree to 3–4in (7.5–10cm).

Fans: Follow the procedure given for peaches on page 137 to create the framework of the tree. In spring, rub out any buds that are growing towards or away from the wall. Pinch the side shoots back to six leaves in mid-summer. When the fruit has been harvested, cut back the side shoots by half. In subsequent years, little further pruning will be necessary.

Propagation: By budding or grafting.

Harvesting and storing: Pick dessert plums when ripe. They will only keep for a few days. Harvest culinary varieties when they are slightly underripe. Plums can be frozen, but remove the stones first.

Average yields:
Standard: 45–100lb (20.5–45.5kg)
Half-standard: 25-60lb (11.3–27.2kg)
Fan: 12–24lb (5.4–11kg)
Bush: 25–50lb (11.3–23kg)
Pyramid: 25–50lb (11.3–23kg)

Pests and diseases: Aphids, apple twig cutter, plum sawfly maggots, caterpillars, bacterial canker, shot hole disease, silver leaf disease.

Recommended varieties:
'Early Prolific' (organic) is an early ripening, dark purple plum that is a good dessert fruit.
'Victoria' (organic) is a popular variety with pale red skin and yellowish-green flesh. A reliable, heavy cropper.
'Oullins Gage' (organic) is a vigorous, self-fertile variety that bears large, round, gage-like fruits with greenish-yellow skins and flesh.

Companion plants: Tansy, garlic.

ABOVE **Plum 'Victoria'**

NAME: **POMEGRANATE**
PUNICA GRANATUM
FAMILY: **PUNICACEAE / MORACEAE**

Type: Perennial

USDA zone: 9–10

Description: The pomegranate has deciduous, glossy, dark green leaves and orange-sized, leathery skinned fruit, which is red-tinged and shiny. The juice is packed in sacs around each seed. Most cultivars are self-fertile.

Where to grow: Pomegranates prefer a well-drained, heavy loam (pH about 7) but will grow on practically any type of soil. They like a sunny, sheltered site and are well adapted to regions with hot, dry summers. They can be grown under glass and in containers.

When to plant: Plant bare-root plants from spring to autumn. Plant container-grown plants at any time if the weather is suitable.

How to grow: Sow seed in compost-filled trays. It will germinate within six weeks. Thin the seedlings and harden them off then plant outdoors at the same distances as rooted cuttings. Rooted cuttings and suckers can also

be planted outdoors, 12–20ft (3.6–6m) apart each way. The young plants can be grown in greenhouse borders or in containers. The pomegranate can be trained as a small tree, but is more commonly grown as a bushy shrub.

Maintenance: Weed regularly and water frequently in dry weather. Apply a general fertilizer every two or three months once the plants are established. Cut out all suckers.

Pruning and training: Select three or four main branches to form the framework and cut out any diseased, crowded, crossing or dead branches. Remove suckers regularly to train the plant into tree form, beginning soon after planting. The bush tree form will develop naturally.

Propagation: From seed. Seedlings, however, do not come true to type. Also by air layering and by hardwood cuttings taken in late winter/early spring. Root suckers can be taken from the parent plant and replanted.

Harvesting and storing: The fruits will be ready for harvesting from summer until autumn. Harvest when they turn yellow or red. They are usually eaten fresh, but can be stored for a few weeks at a temperature of 39–43°F (4–6°C)

Average yields: Difficult to estimate. Fruit production increases with the size of the plant.

Pests and diseases: Few when grown outdoors. Under glass they can be troubled by red spider mite, thrips, aphids, whitefly and fungal disease.

Recommended varieties:

'Wonderful' is a Californian variety.

'Nana' is a hardier, dwarf variety ideal for container growing.

'Purple Seed' and 'Spanish Ruby' are popular varieties in Florida.

Companion plants: None known.

ABOVE **A young pomegranate growing**

NAME: **PRICKLY PEAR** *(OPUNTIA SPP)* FAMILY: **CACTACEAE**

Type: Evergreen

USDA zone: 5–10 (depending on species)

Description: Prickly pear, also known as prickly pear cactus, thrives in dry Mediterranean areas. It has round or oval, thick, fleshy pads covered with tufts of spines and bears both male and female flowers from mid/late summer which are pollinated by insects. Its fruits can be red, orange, pink, purple or lime green.

Where to grow: Prickly pears prefer a well-drained, open, limy, soil (pH6–7.5) and a warm, sunny position. A position at the base of a south-facing wall, protected from wind and rain is ideal. They can be grown under glass in cooler climates, and in large pots.

When to plant: Sow seed under glass in early spring. Plant cuttings of leaf pads at any time during the growing season.

How to grow: Sow seed in a well-drained compost in the greenhouse. Prick out seedlings into pots when they are large enough to handle. Harden off and plant in permanent positions in late spring/early summer, when all danger of frost has passed, at up to 15ft (4.5m) apart depending upon their mature size. Grow greenhouse plants on under glass for at least the first two winters.

Maintenance: Prickly pears will tolerate considerable neglect, but should be kept weed free and protected from rain, wind and frost.

Pruning and training: None necessary. The pads may need propping up.

Propagation: From seed, and from detached pads. Remove a pad from the plant and leave it to dry in a warm, sunny place for a few days by which time the base should be thoroughly dry and have begun to form a callus. Pot up in a sandy compost where it will root quickly.

Harvesting and storing: In warm climates, pads

CAUTION

Always wear thick gloves when handling prickly pear plants. The tufts of spines can become embedded in the skin and they are extremely difficult to remove.

can be harvested up to six times a year. Once harvested, the fruits will keep for several days. Remove the thorny peel before eating.

Average yields: Established plants may yield up to forty 8oz (225g) pads at each harvest.

Pests and diseases: No significant problems.

Recommended varieties:

'Blind Prickly Pear' has red, fleshy fruit and grows to up to 6ft (1.8m).

'Purple Prickly Pear' has oblong, bluish-purple pads with long black or white spines. It grows to up to 3.5ft (1.07m).

'Englemann's Prickly Pear' has blue-green, circular or oblong pads and large, juicy, reddish-purple fruit. It grows up to 5ft (1.5m).

Companion plants: None known.

ABOVE **Prickly pear**

147

NAME: **QUINCE**
CYDONIA OBLONGA
FAMILY: **ROSACEAE**

Type: Perennial

USDA zone: 5–9

Description: Quinces are small, bushy trees bearing aromatic, pear- or apple-shaped, yellow fruits covered with downy hairs. The decorative pink and white blossom is similar to apple blossom and appears in summer singly on short shoots. The trees are self-fertile.

Where to grow: Quinces prefer a deep, light, fertile, moisture-retentive and slightly acidic soil, pH6–6.5. A sunny, sheltered site is ideal. In temperate climates, they are usually grown as bushes or fans on south-facing walls. They do well near ponds or streams.

When to plant: Plant bare-rooted trees in autumn or winter. Set out container-grown plants at any time if the weather is suitable.

How to grow: Prepare the ground thoroughly in autumn and add an organic fertilizer. Dig a hole deep and wide enough to take the extended roots and drive in a supporting stake, making sure that it just clears the lowest branches. Support will be needed for the first three years. Plant the tree about 2in from the stake to the same depth as the original soil mark. Make sure the union between the rootstock and the grafted stem (scion) is about 4in (10cm) above ground. Return the soil, firm in well, and tie the tree to the stake with a tree tie. Space standards 20ft (6m) apart, half-standards 15ft (4.5m) apart, and bushes 10–12ft (3–3.6m) apart.

Maintenance: Little needed. Water, mulch and feed established trees occasionally. Keep weed-free and mulch with well-rotted manure in late winter if the soil is poor. Spray with seaweed solution every four weeks.

ABOVE **Quince 'Champion'**

Pruning and training: Quinces are hard to train in the first year. It may be best to buy a two-year-old bush or a three- or four-year-old standard or half-standard. The tree fruits on spurs and on the tips of the previous summer's growth. Prune in winter for the first three–four years, cutting back the leaders of the main framework branches by half of the previous season's growth to an outward facing bud. Prune back crowding side shoots to two or three buds. After the fourth year, very little pruning is needed, although it is important to keep the centre of the bush open. Thin occasionally in winter to remove old, overcrowded growth. Do not prune every lateral because it will remove too many fruit buds.

Propagation: By chip-budding on to 'Quince A' rootstocks in summer, and by hardwood cuttings in the autumn.

Harvesting and storing: The quince crops after 3–4 years. Pick the aromatic fruits in mid-autumn before the first frosts. Store for 4–8 weeks until the skin turns from yellow to green. Store away from other fruit on trays in a cool, dark place.

Average yields: A mature half-standard tree will produce 50lb (23kg) of fruit.

Pests and diseases: Greenfly, sawfly, codling moth, winter moth, woolly aphid, fireblight, mildew, canker, bitter pit, brown rot, wasps, scab.

Recommended varieties:

'Champion' (organic) produces heavy crops of apple-shaped, golden yellow fruit.

'Meech's Prolific' (organic) is a US variety with large flowers and large, pear-shaped fruit.

'Vranja' (organic) has attractive, pink blossom, and very large, golden, pear-shaped fruit.

Companion plants: Pungent herbs like chives and garlic.

NAME: RASPBERRY
RUBUS IDAEUS
FAMILY: ROSACEAE

Type: Perennial

USDA zone: 6–8

Description: Raspberries are a cool season crop. Fruits vary in colour from dark red through to yellow. There are two main types: summer fruiting with a short season of heavy cropping, and autumn fruiting with crops from late summer until the winter frosts. Raspberries are self-fertile.

Where to grow: Raspberries prefer soil that is not too heavy, rich in organic matter and slightly acid (pH6–6.5). It should be well-drained, but also moisture-retentive. Choose a sheltered site, as strong winds can damage the canes and also prevent pollinating insects from visiting. The canes grow best in full sun, but will tolerate partial shade.

ABOVE **Raspberry 'Polka'**

149

When to plant: Plant bare-rooted canes in late autumn/early winter or early spring. Plant container grown plants any time of the year if the weather is suitable.

How to grow: Prepare the soil a month before planting by digging a trench 9in (23cm) deep and 18in (45cm) wide. Spread compost or well-rotted manure over the bottom. At planting time, dig a trench in the prepared soil about 3in (7.5cm) deep and 12–18in (30–45cm) wide and place the canes into it 18in (45cm) apart. Make sure the old soil mark on the canes is level with the surface and spread the roots evenly. Replace the soil and gently tread in the plants. Cut back the stem to a bud 12in (30cm) above soil level. Water in thoroughly. Summer-fruiting varieties will need support.

Maintenance: Water the canes regularly in the first season if the weather is dry and keep the soil moist when the fruit is swelling. Hoe regularly and mulch with well-rotted manure or compost in early spring. In summer, remove suckers and pull out any stems growing away from the canes. For summer fruiting container grown plants, any flowers that appear in the first summer after planting should be removed.

Pruning and training:

Established summer fruiting varieties: After harvesting cut down all the canes that have borne fruit, keeping the best half a dozen unfruited ones which should be tied to the wires at a distance of 3in (7.5cm) apart. In late winter, cut back the tall growth to 6in (15cm) above the top wire.

Established autumn fruiting varieties: Cut down all the canes to ground level in late winter. As the new canes grow in spring, tie them to the wires.

Propagation: By suckers. Choose young healthy canes and remove the plant suckers by cutting them away from the parent root. Plant them in their new growing position.

Harvesting and storing: Pick the fruit when firm but not too ripe for freezing or jam making. Pick it when it is fully ripe for eating straight away. Try to harvest the berries every two days if possible.

Average yields: Summer fruiting: 4.5lb (2.kg) per 3ft (90cm) of row. Autumn fruiting: 1.5lb (675g) per 3ft (90cm) of row.

Possible pests and diseases: Raspberry beetle, greenfly, birds, raspberry moth, cane spot, spur blight, grey mould.

Recommended varieties:

Early/Mid season: 'Malling Jewel' (organic) bears lovely, juicy fruit and tolerates most conditions.

'Glen Rosa' (organic) has a distinctive, aromatic flavour and smaller fruits than 'Malling Jewel'. Ideal for organic growing.

Autumn: 'Autumn Bliss' (organic) crops on first year canes from late summer until the first frosts.

Companion plants: Parsley, tansy.

NAME: STRAWBERRY
FRAGARIA X ANANASSA
FAMILY: ROSACEAE

Type: Perennial

USDA zone: 9–11

Description: Strawberries have luscious, red berries and a delicious, sweet flavour. The plants are self-fertile and remain productive only for about three years.

Where to grow: Strawberries enjoy a humus-rich, moisture-retentive, slightly acid soil and an open, sunny site. A light soil will ensure early crops. They can be grown in containers.

When to plant:

Summer fruiting varieties: Plant bare-rooted plants from mid-summer to early autumn. May also be planted in early spring.

Perpetual varieties: Plant in mid to late summer or in early spring.

Alpine varieties: Sow seed in autumn.

How to grow:

Summer fruiting varieties: Plant 18in (45cm) apart in rows 30in (75cm) apart. If planted in early spring, remove the flowers in the first season.

Perpetual varieties: Plant 18in (45cm) apart in rows 30in (75cm) apart. If planted in early spring, remove the flowers in the first season.

Alpine varieties: Overwinter in an unheated greenhouse. Plant out in mid spring 12in (30cm) apart in rows 24in (60cm) apart.

Maintenance: Water regularly during the first few weeks after planting and in dry spells. Keep water away from the ripening berries. When the berries begin to swell cover the ground beneath them with straw and protect from birds. After cropping, cut off old leaves and runners surplus to requirements about 3in (7.5cm) above the crowns. Rake up any debris, including the straw. Fork up any compacted soil between the rows, leaving the ground free from weeds.

Pruning: Prune when fruiting has finished.

Propagation:

Summer fruiting varieties: Bury small compost-filled pots. Peg runners from cropping plants into them. They should root in four to six weeks. Sever the plantlets from the runners and remove the wire pegging. Plant out into their new position and water well.

Perpetual varieties: Some varieties produce runners and are propagated in the same way as summer fruiting ones. Others are propagated by division, and planted in their new position immediately after dividing.

Harvesting and storing: Pick the fruit as it ripens with a short piece of stalk attached. Eat fresh, bottle or freeze, or make into jam.

Average yields: 6–24oz (170–675g) per plant.

Pests and diseases: Strawberry blossom weevil, slugs, snails, birds, squirrels, beetles, strawberry seed beetle, strawberry mildew, crown rot, wilt.

Recommended varieties:

Summer fruiting:

Early: 'Mae' (organic) produces heavy crops of firm, large fruits.

Mid season: 'Alice' (organic) has sweet, even sized fruit, and excellent disease resistance.

Late season: 'Florence' (organic) gives high yields of quality fruit.

Perpetual: 'Flamenco' is a heavy cropper with excellent fruit quality.

Companion plants: Parsley, spinach, marigolds, lettuce, borage, chives, lavender, onions, sage.

ABOVE **Strawberry 'Royal Sovereign' plant**
INSET **Ripe, juicy berries**

NAME: **SWEET (SPANISH) CHESTNUT (CASTANEA SATIVA)**
FAMILY: **FAGACEAE**

Type: Perennial

USDA zone: 5–9

Description: The sweet chestnut is grown both for its nuts and its timber and makes a massive tree with large, serrated-edged leaves and long, yellow male flowers. It bears prickly burrs that enclose one to three nuts. There are two types: marron and domestic. Sweet chestnuts are rarely self-fertile. They are wind-pollinated, but some cultivars may need a pollinator.

Where to grow: The sweet chestnut enjoys a sandy fertile and moisture-retentive soil (pH6). It grows well in a partially shaded, open, sheltered position. It is not suitable for small gardens as it can grow to 100ft (30m) tall.

When to plant: Plant in autumn or early winter.

How to grow: Buy a one- or two-year-old tree, allowing a planting distance of 30–40ft (9–12m) between trees. Clear an area 5–6ft (1.5–1.8m) square in autumn. Dig in plenty of well-rotted manure and return the soil. At planting time, dig a hole deep and wide enough to take the roots of the tree when fully extended. Drive in a tall stake, leaving about 7ft (2.1m) above the ground. Plant the tree to the same depth as the original soil mark and refill the hole. Tie the tree to the stake with a tree tie. Water in well.

ABOVE **Sweet chestnut**

CAUTION

Do not confuse sweet chestnut trees with horse chestnut. Horse chestnut is entirely different and its fruit is not to be eaten.

Maintenance: Keep the trees weed-free and water when young. Applications of fertilizer will be unnecessary on well-prepared, organically enriched ground.

Pruning and training: Train as a central-leader standard. Little pruning is needed after the main branch system has formed. Once the tree is established, remove dead, diseased, crossed and congested branches as necessary.

Propagation: By bud-grafting or whip-and-tongue grafting on to sweet chestnut seedling rootstocks.

Harvesting and storing: The trees bear nuts after about four years. Harvest them in autumn, hull them and soak for two days. Dry thoroughly and store in a cool place.

Average yields: A 30–60 year old tree can yield 198lb (90kg) of nuts a year. A 50–60 year old tree can yield 594lb (270kg).

Pests and diseases: Birds, squirrels, chestnut blight, leaf spot, honey fungus.

Recommended varieties:

'Dore du Lyons' ripens in mid autumn and has large, round, light-coloured nuts.

'Chinese chestnut' has relatively thin skin and a good flavour.

'Japanese chestnut' is a fairly small sweet chestnut that grows to 40ft (12m) and is highly resistant to chestnut blight.

Companion plants: Grow near oak trees.

NAME: **WALNUT**
JUGLANS REGIA
FAMILY: **JUGLANDACEAE**

Type: Perennial

USDA zone: 5–8

Description: Walnuts are slow growing, but make enormous trees that can reach a height of 60ft (18m). The leaves have a sweet, aromatic scent and the fruits have a green husk around them and a wrinkled kernel when opened. The trees will not crop for 5–10 years after planting.

Where to grow: Walnut trees enjoy a deep, heavy, fertile, well-drained soil (pH of 6.5–7) but they will tolerate some alkalinity. The young shoots and flowers can be damaged by spring frosts, so an open situation with shelter is ideal.

When to plant: Late autumn or winter.

How to grow: Choose young trees, which are usually grown as central-leader standards, and plant in prepared ground. Dig a hole wide and deep enough to take the roots when spread out, and drive in a stake that reaches to just below the lowest branches. Plant to the original soil level with the trees 40–60ft (12–18m) apart. Refill the hole and tie the tree to the stake with a tree tie. Water well.

Maintenance: Weed regularly and water when the weather is dry. Mulch to preserve moisture and keep the weeds down. Walnut trees are usually slow to establish, with stronger growth occurring after about three years.

Pruning and training: Very little pruning is required. Prune in mid-winter during dormancy, removing any strong shoots that are awkwardly placed so that you have a framework of evenly spaced branches. Once the head of the tree has formed, pruning will be confined to cutting out diseased or dead branches in late summer.

Propagation: By whip-and-tongue grafting or chip-budding. In cooler climates, keep the grafted tree under glass until the graft has taken.

Harvesting and storing: Pick up the walnuts from the ground and remove the husks. Scrub them with a soft brush and spread them out in a warm place to dry. Pack them in alternate layers of a mixture of dry peat and salt and store in a cool, dry shed or garage for up to six months.

Average yields: 50lb (23kg) per mature tree.

Pests and diseases: Squirrels, bacterial leaf blotch and blight, honey fungus.

Recommended varieties:

'Broadview' is a self-fertile variety.

'Buccaneer' is also self-fertile.

'Mayette' is a vigorous tree with large, round, tapering nuts.

Companion plants: None known.

CAUTION
Plant away from other garden plants because the leaves give off a scent that can prevent seed from germinating.

Wear gloves to reove husks as walnut juice will stain the hands brown.

ABOVE **Walnuts ready to eat**

Glossary of gardening terms

ACID With a pH value of below 7. Acid soil is deficient in lime and basic minerals.

ACCLIMATIZE Accustom plants to a different climate or conditions.

ALKALINE With a pH value above 7.

ANNUAL Plant grown from seed that germinates, flowers, seeds and dies in one growing season.

ANTHER Pollen-containing part of stamen.

ANTHRACNOSE Fungal diseases that thrive in warm rainy weather and cause die-back, twig cankering, spotted, dropping leaves and dead spots on fruit.

BARE-ROOT Dormant plants sold with the soil removed from around the roots.

BIENNIAL A plant that completes its life cycle in two years. It produces stems and leaves in the first year, flowers in the second, then sets seed and dies.

BOLTING Premature flower or seed production.

BREASTWOOD The forward-growing shoots of trees that are trained against support systems.

BUDDING Grafting that is carried out by inserting a single bud into a rootstock.

BUDSTICK Shoot of the current season's growth used for budding.

CALLUS Protective scar tissue formed by plants over a pruning cut or at the base of a cutting.

CAMBIUM Cellular plant tissue responsible for increasing girth of stems and roots.

CHIP-BUDDING Grafting method in which a chip of ripe wood from the rootstock is replaced with a bud-containing chip from the scion.

CHITTING Germinating seed before planting.

COLD FRAME Unheated structure that is used to protect plants in winter.

COLT A semi-vigorous rootstock useful for larger, fan-trained trees.

COMPANION PLANT A plant that has a beneficial effect on a plant growing nearby.

CORDON Tree trained into a single vertical or oblique stem against a wall.

COMPOST
1 A growing medium that contains ingredients such as peat, loam, sand and leaf mould.
2 Recycled, decomposed plant or other organic matter used to improve soil or as a mulch.

CULTIVAR A cultivated variety of a plant, rather than one that grows naturally in the wild.

DAMPING OFF Disease that attacks seedlings and makes them rot.

DECIDUOUS Loses leaves at the end of every growing season and renews them at the start of the next.

DORMANCY Resting period of a seed or plant when growth temporarily slows or ceases.

DOUBLE DIG Dig soil to a depth equal to the depth of two spade blades.

DRILL Straight furrow made for sowing seed.

ESPALIER Tree trained as a main vertical stem with three or more tiers of branches horizontally in pairs on either side.

EVERGREEN Plants, mainly shrubs and trees, that keep most of their leaves all year round, though some leaves are lost throughout the year.

FAN Tree/bush trained in the shape of a fan.

FEATHERED Year-old trees with lateral shoots.

FRIABLE Term used to describe easily-worked soil of a crumbly texture that is capable of forming a tilth.

GENUS Group of plants with similar characteristics, regarded as a family.

GERMINATION Changes that occur as a seed starts to grow and the root and shoot emerge.

GRAFT Propagate by inserting the scion of one plant into another plant (the stock).

GRAFT UNION Junction of scion and rootstock.

HABIT Characteristic shape and appearance.

HALF-HARDY Will over-winter outside in a sheltered position but may not survive frosts.

HARDEN OFF Acclimatize young plants gradually to outside temperatures.

HARDWOOD CUTTINGS Cuttings taken from mature wood at the end of the growing season.

HARDY Able to survive the winter outdoors without protection.

HEEL IN Plant temporarily until conditions allow the plant to be moved to its permanent position.

HUMUS Crumbly, dark brown, decayed vegetable matter formed by the partial breakdown of plant remains by bacteria.

HYBRID Plant created from parents of different species or genera.

INFLORESCENCE A semi-vigorous rootstock useful for larger, fan-trained trees.

LATERALS Fruit-producing sideshoots.

LAYERING Method of propagation in which a stem is pegged down and encouraged to root while still attached to the parent plant.

LEADER The main, usually central, stem of a plant, or the terminal shoot of a main branch.

LIME Compounds of calcium. The proportion of lime in soil determines its acidity or alkalinity.

LOAM Soil composed of an even mixture of clay and sand, with a balanced mix of nutrients.

MAIDEN A year-old tree.

MAYPOLE Support laden branches using ropes tied to a stake that is attached to the main trunk.

MISTING Fine spraying of plants to prevent dehydration when humidity drops.

MULCH Layer of material applied to soil surface to conserve moisture, improve its structure, protect roots from frost, and suppress weeds.

NUTRIENTS Minerals used to develop proteins and other compounds necessary for the growth and well-being of a plant.

PEAT Partly-decayed organic matter used in growing composts or mulches. Substitutes may be used for environmental reasons.

PERENNIAL A plant that lives for at least three seasons. It flowers annually, dies down in winter, and new shoots appear each spring. Woody-based perennials die down only partially.

PETIOLE The stalk of a leaf.

pH SCALE A scale measured from 1–14 that indicates the alkalinity or acidity of soil. pH 7 is neutral; below pH 7 acid, and above pH 7 alkaline.

PINCH OUT Remove growing tips to encourage side shoot production. Also known as 'stopping'.

POLLINATE Transfer pollen from the male part of the flower (anther) to the female part (stigma).

POME FRUITS Fruit with a pip-containing central core, for example apples.

POTASH Form of potassium that is contained in soil and fertilizers and used by plants.

POT ON Transfer a plant to a larger pot.

PRICK OUT Transfer seedlings from where they germinated to pots or beds.

PROPAGATE Increase plants vegetatively or by seed.

RHIZOME Branched underground stem that bears roots and shoots.

ROOTSTOCK Part of a tree that becomes the root system of a grafted or budded tree.

SCION Piece of the previous season's growth with three or four buds.

SEED LEAVES (COTYLEDONS) The frst pair of leaves that appear after germination.

SELF-FERTILE Term used for a plant that does not need another plant of the same variety planted nearby for pollination.

SELF-STERILE Term used for a plant that needs another plant of the same variety nearby for pollination to take place.

SOFTWOOD CUTTINGS Cuttings taken from young plants during the growing season.

SPECIES Plants of a specific type and constant character that breed together. Seed-grown species are consistently true to type.

SPUR Slow-growing short branch system usually carrying clusters of fruit buds.

SPUR-BEARER Fruit tree that bears most of its fruit on spurs.

STAMEN Male, pollen-bearing flower organ.

STANDARD Tree pruned to give 6–7ft (1.8–2.1m) of clear stem.

STEP-OVER Tree or bush on a very dwarfing rootstock that is trained to produce a single branch on either side of the main stem.

STIGMA Pollen-receiving female flower organ.

SUB-LATERAL Side-shoot from a maiden lateral.

SUBSOIL Soil beneath the top layer or topsoil.

SUCKER Shoot growing from a stem or root at or below ground level.

T-BUDDING Method of grafting using a T-shaped slit in the rootstock.

TENDER Susceptible to damage at low temperatures (cannot survive outside during winter).

THIN Reduce the number of fruitlets.

TILTH Soil broken down into small crumbs by correct digging and raking to form an ideal, fine, crumbly, top layer of soil.

TIP-BEARER Fruit tree that bears most of its fruit on one-year-old shoots.

TIP-LAYERING Method of propagation in which a young, vigorous shoot tip is buried 3–4in (7–10cm) deep in the soil in summer. When a new shoot has developed from the tip it is separated from the parent plant, and transplanted or potted up the following spring.

TOPSOIL The fertile, uppermost layer of soil in which most plants root.

TRIPLOID Term used to describe a plant that has three basic sets of chromosomes. Triploids are usually sterile.

TRUE LEAVES Adult leaves which appear after the seed leaves.

VARIETY Term used to describe a variant of an original species or hybrid, often used for variants induced by cultivation (cultivars).

VENEER GRAFTING Method of propagation carried out on dormant plants. It is done by cutting down through the cambium layer of the rootstock, then making a sloping cut towards the base of the first cut and removing the chip. The scion is shaped to match and the two bound together with clear tape and protected until shoots develop.

WHIP AND TONGUE Grafting done by making matching sloping cuts on the rootstock and scion, then cutting shallow tongues to enable the scion to interlock firmly with the stock.

Index

Pages highlighted in bold include illustrations of plants

PHOTOGRAPHIC ACKNOWLEDGEMENTS

Photographs © Yvonne Cuthbertson except for:
pages 6–7 and 91: Pastor Robert Jones, Sierra Vista, Arizona US;
pages 122 and 147 (main image): Dianne & David Montague;
pages 109 (inset image) and 131: Anna Montague;
pages 2 (bottom left), 5, 30, 61, 93, 100 (inset image), 102, 104, 105 (inset image), 106, 123, 127, 145, 148, 149 and 152: Stephen Shirley, Victoriana Nursery Garden, Challock, Kent, UK;
pages 2 (top right), 117, 142, 146 and 160: Howard and Pat Jordan, Cyprus Garden Club;
page 105 (main image): Meg Game, Kentish Cobnuts Association, Kent, UK;
page 111 (both images): Bill Clifford, Westmorland Damson Association, Cumbria, UK;
pages 60, 94, 100 (main image), 103, 115, 134, 136, 139 and 151 (inset image):
United States Department of Agriculture;
page 109 (main image), 118, 125, 128, 135 and 143: Forest & Kim Starr, Plant Images of Hawaii;
pages 21 and 121: Dade City Kumquat Festival, Florida, US.

Thanks to David Dale for the loan of his digital camera.

GMC Publications Ltd, 166 High Street, Lewes, East Sussex BN7 1XU, United Kingdom
Tel: 01273 488005 Fax: 01273 402866
www.gmcbooks.com

Contact us for a complete catalogue, or visit our website.